SYMBOLIC COMPUTATION

Artificial Intelligence

Springer Series
SYMBOLIC COMPUTATION - *Artificial Intelligence*

R.S. Michalski, J.G. Carbonell, T.M. Mitchell (Eds.): Machine Learning. An Artificial Intelligence Approach. XI, 572 pages, 1984

A. Bundy (Ed.): Catalogue of Artificial Intelligence Tools. Second, revised edition. IV, 168 pages, 1986

C. Blume, W. Jakob: Programming Languages for Industrial Robots. XIII, 376 pages, 145 figs., 1986

J.W. Lloyd: Foundations of Logic Programming. Second, extended edition. XII, 212 pages, 1987

L. Bolc (Ed.): Computational Models of Learning. IX, 208 pages, 34 figs., 1987

L. Bolc (Ed.): Natural Language Parsing Systems. XVIII, 367 pages, 151 figs., 1987

N. Cercone, G. McCalla (Eds.): The Knowledge Frontier. Essays in the Representation of Knowledge. XXXV, 512 pages, 93 figs., 1987

G. Rayna: REDUCE. Software for Algebraic Computation. IX, 329 pages, 1987

D.D. McDonald, L. Bolc (Eds.): Natural Language Generation Systems. XI, 389 pages, 84 figs., 1988

L. Bolc, M.J. Coombs (Eds.): Expert System Applications. IX, 471 pages, 84 figs., 1988

C.-H. Tzeng: A Theory of Heuristic Information in Game-Tree Search. X, 107 pages, 22 figs., 1988

L. Kanal, V. Kumar (Eds.): Search in Artificial Intelligence. X, 482 pages, 67 figs., 1988

H. Coelho, J. Cotta: Prolog by Example. 304 pages, 62 figs., 1988

H. Abramson, V. Dahl: Logic Grammars. XV, 258 pages, 40 figs., 1989

R. Hausser: Computation of Language. 425 pages, 1989

B. D'Ambrosio: Qualitative Process Theory Using Linguistic Variables. 156 pages, 22 figs., 1989

Bruce D'Ambrosio

Qualitative Process Theory Using Linguistic Variables

With 22 Figures

Springer-Verlag
New York Berlin Heidelberg
London Paris Tokyo Hong Kong

Bruce D'Ambrosio
Department of Computer Science
Oregon State University
Corvallis, OR 97331-4602

Library of Congress Cataloging-in-Publication Data
D'Ambrosio, Bruce.
Qualitative process theory using linguistic variables.
(Symbolic computation. Artificial intelligence)
Includes bibliographical references.
1. Artificial intelligence. 2. Reasoning.
3. Linguistics. I. Title. II. Series.
Q335.D36 1989 006.3 89-21698

Printed on acid-free paper

Camera-ready text prepared by the author using TEX.

9 8 7 6 5 4 3 2 1

ISBN-13: 978-1-4613-9673-4 e-ISBN-13: 978-1-4613-9671-0
DOI: 10.1007/978-1-4613-9671-0

Contents

List of Figures

1

Overview

In this book we explore the use of linguistic variables as a semiquantitative extension to the qualitative value and relationship representations in qualitative process theory, for application in fuzzy logic control. Qualitative process (QP) theory, developed by Kenneth Forbus, describes the form of qualitative theories about the dynamics of physical systems. Its central thesis is that all change in such systems is the result of active processes, and that these processes should be explicitly represented and reasoned about. Much of QP theory's power derives from the qualitative representations used for the values of individual continuous-state parameters and the relations between these parameters. Qualitative descriptions are important because they provide the ability to reason with incomplete information and can guide the application of more detailed quantitative theories when additional information is available. Forbus has demonstrated that QP theory can be used to derive many significant deductions given only weak qualitative descriptions of variable values and relationships. For example, QP theory can be used to determine that the water in Fig. 1.1 will heat up and eventually boil, and that the container may eventually explode. However, there are at least three limitations to the current ability to analyze this situation using QP theory:

1. QP theory cannot be used to estimate how likely it is that there will be an explosion.

2. QP theory is unable to analyze situations only slightly more complicated than the one shown. For example, if we include a model for heat loss from the container to the surrounding environment, QP theory can no longer predict whether or not the water will boil.

3. QP theory provides little basis for reasoning about continuous control actions; for example, how much or when should the heat be turned down to avoid explosion?

We show that QP theory can be extended through the use of linguistic variables [Zad75a] to characterize both quantity magnitudes and necessary aspects of functional relationships. These extensions can reduce the ambiguity of QP analyses in terms of both the number of possible situations that may be occurring and the magnitude, time scale, etc., over which situations occur. These extensions reason at the appropriate level of detail for the kinds of questions typically asked in reasoning about the control of engineered systems; they are computationally tractable and can reason with

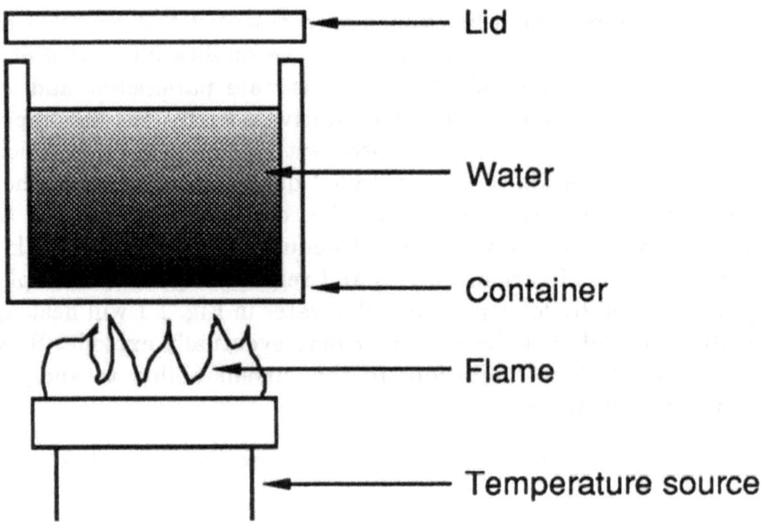

FIGURE 1.1. Boiling Example, after Forbus [For84].

the imprecise or uncertain data typically available to real-world control systems. These extensions are motivated by an examination of the potential use of QP theory in reasoning about the control of an engineered physical system, a chemical reaction furnace. Examination of the detailed model reveals a number of limitations similar to those listed. The source of these limitations is then traced to the restricted model of naive mathematics contained in QP theory. The proposed extensions to this mathematics are then described and demonstrated to be capable of eliminating many of the limitations at the price of requiring additional system-specific information about the system being modeled.

The three extensions presented in this book are based on the notion of a linguistic variable. First, an extension to the truth values and quantity ordering relations in QP theory enables representation of uncertain measurement data and estimates of state likelihoods. Second, an examination of qualitative characterizations of functional relationships reveals a number of possible extensions to the qualitative proportionality and influence relations of QP theory. One in particular, relationship strength, is shown to be capable of resolving some of the ambiguity that arises when attempting to apply QP theory to complex situations. Finally, an extension theory for the quantity representations used by QP theory, when combined with the other described extensions, provides estimates of the quantitative effects of adjustments to continuous control parameters. Much of the information required to improve the specificity of the results of applying QP theory is physical system, state, or even query specific. The work presented here is based on the hypothesis that problem solving does not proceed by choosing a single representation and manipulating it until a solution is found, but rather by choosing an initial representation, performing some initial problemsolving, "patching" the representation in response to problems encountered, and again resuming problem solving. This cycle may iterate several times before a satisfactory solution is reached. "Patches" are applied on the basis of the problems encountered and the query being asked, and are drawn from sources of information outside the theory being applied. We do not address the source of this external information here, but some initial explorations of this question are described in [D'A85].

Chapter 2 introduces the basic notions of fuzzy logic control. Chapter 3 provides a review of QP theory, including background and related research. Chapter 4 then presents an example, in which QP theory is used to analyze a simple continuous-flow industrial chemical system. Chapter 5 examines the results of this analysis, identifies certain limitations of QP theory in reasoning for process control, and analyzes the sources of those limitations. Chapter 5 ends with a description of an approach to addressing these limitations using linguistic variables. Chapter 6 provides some basic review material on linguistic variables, and presents some of the basic machinery needed to support the deductions used in later work. Chapter 7 introduces the concept of a linguistic quantity space, and show it integrates multiple representations of quantity information. Chapter 8 examines the problem of characterization of functional relationships. A number of different kinds of characterizations are identified, and one in particular, the notion of relationship strength, is shown to be capable of resolving one of the undecidable questions exposed in the example in chapters 4 and 5. Chapter 9 discusses the problem of estimating the effects of adjustments to continuous control parameters and presents linguistic perturbation analysis, a technique for producing these estimates for a wide class of situations. Finally, Chapter 10 summarizes the work presented here, compares it with related work, and outlines possibilities for further research.

2

Fuzzy Logic Control

2.1 Classical Control Theory

In this chapter we review previous results in the effort to incorporate approximate reasoning into the control of physical processes. In particular, we wish to review the research in fuzzy logic control and show how the research presented here is a logical extension of that work. Fuzzy control is an outgrowth of classical control theory, so we start with a brief review of classical control.

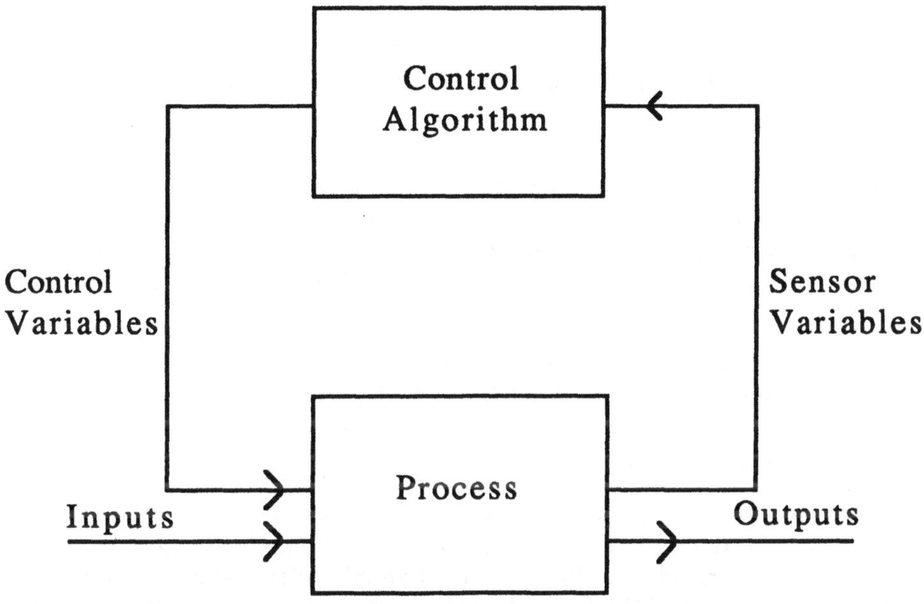

FIGURE 2.1. Classical Model of Process Control

As shown in Fig. 2.1, classical control theory is concerned with four basic components: the process to be controlled, a set of process parameters that can be observed (the sensor or control system input variables), a second set of process parameters that can be directly controlled (called the control or control system output variables), and a control algorithm that transforms sets of sensor variable observations into sets of control variable settings. The control algorithm is derived from a model of the process to be controlled. When the model is accurate and the control algorithm derivation performe(d correctly, the performance and stability of the control algorithm can be guaranteed within known limits. Control theory is well known and understood, and is the control mechanism of choice when applicable. However, in many situations, classical control theory may not be applicable for several reasons:

1. There may be no complete model of the process, or available models may be too complex or make unacceptable assumptions.
2. Control algorithms derived by classical techniques do not respond well to noise in sensor variable measurements [Mur85].
3. The stability and performance available from classical control algorithms may not be adequate for the requirements of the task at hand.

2.2 A New Approach to Control of Complex Systems

Fuzzy logic control was developed to overcome some of the problems cited above. Research on fuzzy control is an outgrowth of a landmark paper by Zadeh [Zad73] outlining a new approach to decision making in complex domains. This approach is based on the *principle of incompatibility*:

> ... as the complexity of a system increases, our ability to make precise yet significant statements about its behavior diminishes until a threshold is reached beyond which precision and significance (or relevance) become almost mutually exclusive characteristics.[1]

In this paper Zadeh introduced the *linguistic variable* to provide approximate descriptions of significant parameter values, the *fuzzy conditional statement* to provide for descriptions of simple relationships between linguistic variables, and the *fuzzy algorithm* to describe more complex relationships. Briefly, a linguisitic variable is a variable whose value is represented as a possibility distribution over a value space (for more details see Chapter 7). Fuzzy algorithms are constructed from fuzzy assignment and fuzzy conditional statements. Particularly relevant in the context of fuzzy control is the *fuzzy relational algorithm* introduced in [Zad73]. A fuzzy relational algorithm describes the relationship between fuzzy variables and is defined

[1] See [Zad73], p. 28.

as a set of conditional statements. Fuzzy relational algorithms can express the relationship between two or more variables, as well as the relationships between different aspects of the variables involved. Following is an example from [Zad73] describing the relationship between the value and first derivative of the variable x and the first derivative of the variable y:

Algorithm F(x, y):

1. **If** x is *small* and x is increased *slightly*, **then** y will increase *slightly*.
2. **If** x is *small* and x is increased *substantially*, **then** y will increase *substantially*.
3. **If** x is *large* and x is increased *slightly*, **then** y will increase *moderately*.
4. **If** x is *large* and x is increased *substantially*, **then** y will increase *very substantially*.

In the case in which multiple rules apply, each serves to restrict the possible value of the consequent, and therefore Zadeh recommends that the proper combining rule is to intersect the results.

2.3 Fuzzy Control

Mamdani [MA75], [Mam76] was the first to apply the ideas presented in Zadeh's paper to the problem of process control. Mamdani encountered the problem that classical control theory was often inapplicable, usually because of lack of a suitable formal model of the process. However, there was available a large body of vague, nonnumeric information about how to control the process of interest, a simple steam engine in his first study. Mamdani found that fuzzy relational algorithms provided a direct representation for this knowledge, and that the defined semantics of fuzzy relational algorithms, when applied to these representations, determined control actions that corresponded with the control actions performed by skilled operators. The new model of control proposed by Mamdani is shown in Fig. 2.2 and is considerably different from the standard model of control.[2]

The process, sensor parameters, and control parameters are as before. Sensor readings, which are assumed to be nonfuzzy, must be converted to fuzzy set form, and this occurs in a process called *fuzzification*. The definitions of the fuzzy predicates are stored in a *database* associated with the controller. The linguistic control knowledge is stored as a set of fuzzy conditional statements in a *rule-base* and can be seen as specifying a fuzzy

[2] Figure adapted from [Ton84].

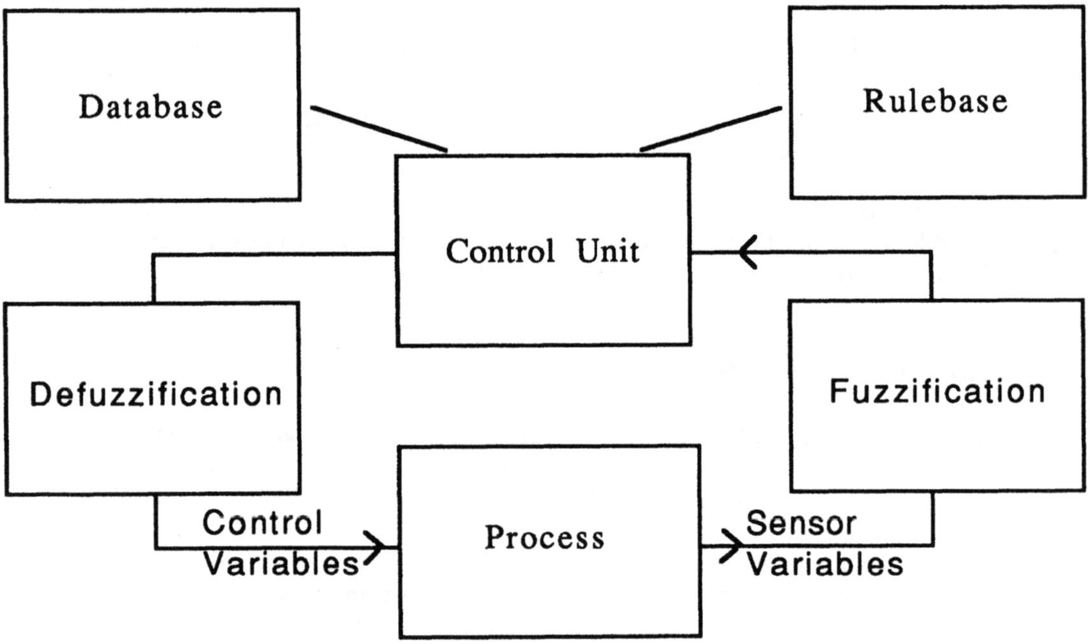

FIGURE 2.2. A Model of Fuzzy Logic Control

relational control algorithm. The ***computation unit*** combines the ***fuzzified sensor data*** with the ***database*** and the ***rule-base*** to determine a ***fuzzy action specification***. Finally, this is converted to a specific nonfuzzy control action in the ***action interface***. Tong [Ton84] points out that one assumption behind this model is that the condition part of the fuzzy conditional control statements will refer to sensor parameters and their rates of change, and that the action parts will refer to control parameters or their increments. Fuzzy logic control can be seen, then, as an attempt to extend the classical control ideas. There are, however three new algorithms required for fuzzy logic control, namely; those for ***fuzzification*** of the input, for ***rule interpretation***, and for ***defuzzification*** of the output. We now review each of these.

2.3.1 Fuzzification of Input

Sensor input can be in two forms. Direct instrument measurements are usually nonfuzzy real values. Alternatively, human observations are often expressed as linguistic values. In either case, the goal is to convert these to discrete fuzzy sets. The problem of converting a linguistic term into a fuzzy set of discrete elements of a ***basis set*** is discussed in the chapter on linguistic variables. When the input is numeric, it can be converted to a fuzzy singleton:[3]

$$S = 1.0/(R - mod(R, d))$$

where R is the real-valued sensor measurement and d the increment between adjacent values in the basis set.[4]

2.3.2 Rule Interpretation

Rule interpretation consists of two stages. The first is interpretation of individual rules, and the second is combination of the results of multiple rules. Individual rule interpretation is performed using the compositional rule of inference, as outlined in the chapter on linguistic variables. Specifically, the consequences of

If X is a **then** Y is b

Given that X is measured to be a', can be computed via

$$Y = a' * (aXb)$$

$$Y = \sum_j \vee_i \wedge u_{a'}(i) \wedge u_a(i) u_b(j)$$

[3]from [Lar85].

[4]This assumes that this increment is constant, usually the case in existing applications of fuzzy logic control.

This extends naturally for compound antecedents:

If X is a **then if** Y is b **then** Z is C

can be evaluated as follows, given that X is observed to be a' and Y is observed to be b':

$$Z = b' * (a' * (aXbXc))$$

$$Z = \sum_{k} \vee_{i,j} \wedge u_{A'}(i) u_A(i) u_{B'}(j) u_B(j) u_C(k)$$

Notice that this formulation of the representation of the fuzzy conditional statements does not include a term of the form $\neg a' X v$ and therefore represents the support for possible values of the consequent, given information about the antecedents, rather than a restriction on possible values of the consequent. Therefore, a natural combining rule for multiple fuzzy conditional statements is the union operator, and this is in fact what Mamdani and most other workers in fuzzy logic control use:

Given a series of rules that conclude about a variable Y, of the form:

If X is a_1 **then** Y is b_1
If X is a_2 **then** Y is b_2
If X is a_3 **then** Y is b_3
etc.

And given that X is measured to be a', then Y can be computed via

$$Y = \vee_k (a' * (a_k X b_k)$$

$$Y = \sum_{j,k} \vee_i \wedge u_{a'}(i) \wedge u_{a_k}(i) u_{b_k}(j)$$

2.3.3 Defuzzification

The output of this step is a fuzzy set of possible control actions. A final algorithm is necessary in order to choose a single nonfuzzy action to perform on the system to be controlled. Zadeh proposed in [Zad73] the *rule of the preponderant alternative* which, simply stated, specifies the selection of the alternative with the highest degree of membership. In some cases, however, the membership function for the possible control action may be bimodal or have a wide plateau, as shown in Fig. 2.3.

In these cases the original paper by Mamdani [MA75] recommends selecting the action midway between the two peaks or at the center of the plateau. Larkin [Lar85], however, compares this to a *center-of-area* approach and shows that for at least one experiment in fuzzy flight control, COA produces a smoother response pattern. The center-of-area V^* of a membership function Y' is

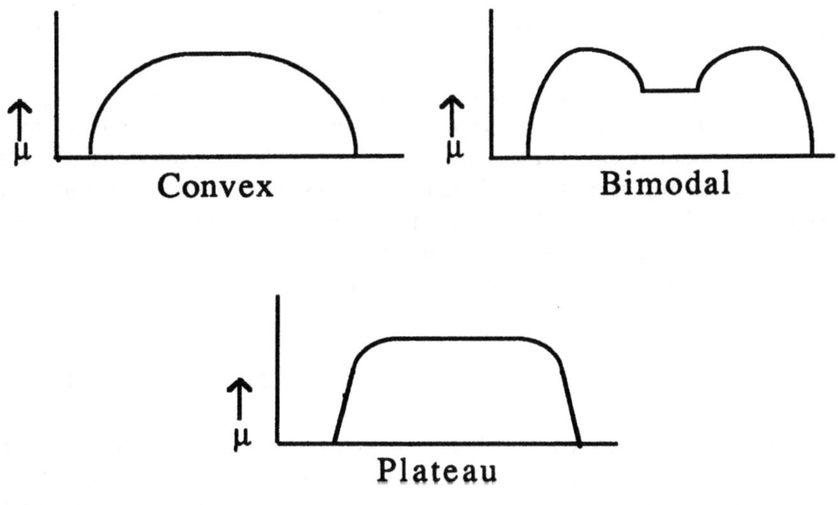

FIGURE 2.3. Possible Membership Functions for Fuzzy Control Actions

$$V^* = \frac{\sum j = 1, n v_j u_{Y'}(v_j)}{\vee B_{j=1,n} u_{Y'}(v_j)}$$

The original papers by Mamdani spurred considerable interest in fuzzy logic control and resulted in attempts to apply the ideas in a number of application areas, including Ostergaard's work on control of a cement kiln [HO82], which eventually became a commercial product, Kickert and van Nauta Lemke's application to control of a warm water plant [KvNL76], and Tong's application of fuzzy control to wastewater treatment [Ton80]. Mamdani's [MA75] original work applied fuzzy logic control to the control of a steam engine and boiler. Simulation results showed it to be faster than a direct digital control algorithm in response to disturbances from equilibrium. Larkin [Lar85] found smoother response to a noisy environment. Yasunobu and Miyamoto [YM85] demonstrated smoother response, closer maintenance of tolerances, and lower energy use from a predictive fuzzy controller for automatic train operation, when compared with a traditional control approach. A substantial amount of more theoretical work was also initiated, including the study of such problems as the stability and reliability of fuzzy logic controllers. A major unresolved theoretical question is that of determining whether or not the controller will determine a response for all possible situations that it might encounter.

2.4 Extensions of the Fuzzy Control Paradigm

Previous work in fuzzy control has achieved considerable success in using the fuzzy relational algorithm to directly express expert control knowledge in an operational form, as we have seen. However, it has been found to be quite difficult to acquire the requisite control knowledge [Ton84]. This is similar to the situation in rule-based expert systems, where the ***knowledge acquisition bottleneck*** is widely recognized. Tong [Ton85] has suggested that a move to adopt some of the techniques of rule-based systems would benefit fuzzy control and somewhat alleviate the knowledge acquisition problem. Specifically, he recommends abandoning the restriction of relating output parameters directly to input parameters, and suggests the use of a more complex conceptual model, which includes intermediate state parameters, as a way of factoring knowledge acquisition.

An alternate approach has been pursued by Yasunobu and Miyamoto [YM85]. They constructed a fuzzy relational model of the system to be controlled and then made control decisions by choosing the control action that performed best in the model. In particular, they start with a set of control rules of the form

If (U is $c_i \rightarrow X$ is a_i and Y is b_i) **then** U is c_i

where X and Y are fuzzy process models of the form[5]:

$$u_X(t_c, N_c) = \mathbf{A}(t_c, N_c, -N_c + C_b)$$

then a control action can be determined by a two-part process. First, the validity of each control rule must be evaluated in the current environment, and then the most valid rule must have its action part evaluated. The validity V of control rule i at time t is determined as follows:

$$V_i(t) = (a_i \wedge X(c_i, t)) * (b_i \wedge Y(c_i, t))$$

and the action recommendation of the selected rule is computed by

$$Action_i = \vee u_{rule-i}(C_i : x, y) \mid t$$

However, note that the fuzzy models used by Yasunobu and Miyamoto retain the simple input/output relationship criticized by Tong and may be as difficult to acquire as direct control knowledge.

2.5 The Next Step: Fuzzy-Model-Based Control

In fuzzy-model-based control we present a similar approach, but allow a more complex representation of the process model, as suggested by Tong. In particular, we will use qualitative process (QP) theory as the basic process modeling tool. The reasons for choosing such a complex modeling tool have already been discussed, but it must be noted here that the complex process models that can be constructed using QP theory do not lend themselves to use in the simple direct fashion of [YM85]. Rather, we adopt a more structured view of the problem of process control, adapted from that first elucidated for medical diagnosis by such systems as EMYCIN [BS84] and CASNET [Wei84]. That is, we factor the process control problem into two phases, ***situation assessment*** and ***response planning***. Situation assessment is the process of constructing high-level linguistic characterizations of the state of the process in terms that are directly relevant to process management, and response planning is the process of determining an appropriate action, given an assessment of the current state and a goal description. Figure 2.4 shows the structure we have in mind, where the fuzzy process model is a key resource in both interpreting sensor data and selecting appropriate responses.

In the next few chapters we introduce QP theory and show how it could potentially serve as the model-based reasoning component of a fuzzy-logic

---

[5] **A** is a parameterized generic fuzzy-set membership function. Note that the fuzzy models can include input variables other than the one being considered (N_c in the above case). For further details see [YM85].

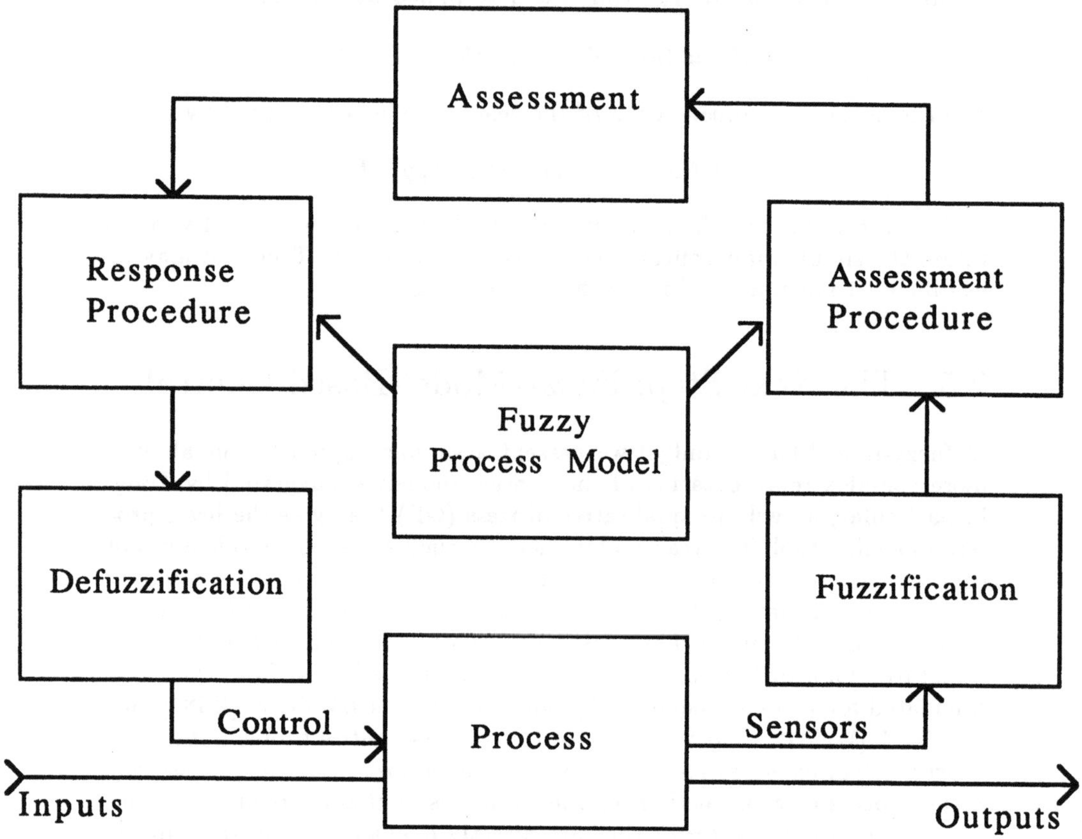

FIGURE 2.4. Fuzzy-Model-Based Control

controller. QP theory already has a mechanism of situation assessment, called ***measurement interpretation***, within it. However, as we shall show, this mechanism is severely limited by the impoverished representations used in QP theory. We shall show how this mechanism can be extended to take advantage of the additional fuzzy process model knowledge we can capture and, as a result, produce useful situation assessments with less information than previously required.

We are not primarily concerned with the second phase of our extended model of process control, response planning. Nonetheless, we shall also show how another technique, linguistic perturbation (LP) analysis, can be extended to answer linguistic "what if" questions. This technique can then be used directly as the modeling component of a Yasunobu-like predictive controller, or as a plan checker to verify the consequences of proposed control actions.

3

Introduction to Qualitative Process Theory

Reasoning about physical systems requires the integration of a range of knowledge and reasoning techniques. P. Hayes has named the enterprise of identifying and formalizing the common-sense knowledge people use for this task "naive physics." Qualitative process (QP) theory by K. Forbus proposes a structure and some of the content of naive theories about dynamics (i.e., the way things change in a physical situation). Classical physics, along with its foundations in real mathematics and especially differential calculus, has been under development for thousands of years and is a very sophisticated and successful tool for analyzing the physical world. What, then, is the motivation for pursuing qualitative modeling techniques? There are two basic motivations behind the work in qualitative physics:

1. To see how much can be derived from very weak descriptions of a physical situation. Often, we may not have precise measurements of masses, positions, velocities, etc.

2. To reduce the amount of preanalysis that must be performed before theory can be applied.

To satisfy the first goal, qualitative physics has adopted the modeling approach of linear systems theory [Coc80], adapted to a qualitative range [−, 0, +] for continuous parameters. In [dKB84b], de Kleer and Brown outline the qualitative analogs of several basic components of the differential calculus, including the notion of continuity, the mean value theorem, and Rolle's theorem. Further formalization of the foundations of qualitative mathematics and qualitative differential analysis can be found in [dKB84a], [Sac85], and [Wil88]. An additional potential advantage of this approach is that solutions can readily be found to the qualitative analogs of complex nonlinear systems that defy real analysis.

But improving the ability to analyze situations for which only weak information is available is only one, and perhaps the lesser, of the goals of qualitative physics. The goal listed earlier is to reduce the amount of preanalysis needed. One way to do this is to identify and formalize the "prephysics" knowledge or set of unstated assumptions on which most of modern physics is based. We can identify five steps in the analysis of any physical situation:

1. Choose an appropriate theory for analyzing the problem (e.g., thermodynamics or statics).

2. Segment the situation into objects to be considered, basing the segmentation on the ontology defined in the theory (e.g., a round ball full of liquid might be a single object for a statics analysis, but two separate objects for a thermodynamic analysis).

3. Formulate a model of the situation in terms of the objects identified and the relationships between the objects defined in the theory.

4. Operate on or transform the model in some way.

5. Interpret the transformed (solved) model in terms of the original situation.

Classical physics provides a set of theories that can be chosen in step 1 and mathematics provides a variety of sets of operations that can be applied in step 4. Also, some guidance is provided in step 5. For example, closed-form solutions of feedback situations can be examined and categorized as diverging or converging. However, physics traditionally has not considered the formalization of steps 1, 2, or 3. The physicist must explicitly decide what theory to apply and which objects will be considered, and then manually construct the situation model by selecting and instantiating the appropriate laws from the theory chosen. Also, the physicist must select the appropriate solution method to be applied to the model thus constructed.

De Kleer's formulation of a qualitative physics based on components provides a significant advance in that it automates steps 3 and 4. Once the relevant set of objects is selected, Envision, de Kleer's implementation of his qualitative physics, automatically constructs and solves the situation model. However, Envision still relies on the person describing some situation to specify all the objects that may be relevant, either initially, or during the course of evolution of the situation. Objects that may come into existence during the course of evolution of a physical situation must be explicitly allowed for in advance by the builder of both a standard physical model of a situation and an Envision-style qualitative model. A major contribution in QP theory is the start of automation of step 2, the identification of the relevant objects in a situation. To see why this might be important, imagine the following scenario: A robot is attempting to reason about the construction of some artifact out of flat sheets of material to solve some problem it has encountered. During the course of construction, it assembles as one subassembly an open-topped cube. What would lead it to suspect that this assembly might function as a container, and that, if there is a source of fluid nearby (e.g., rainfall), it might fill with liquid? Since the robot is engaged in an unplanned constructive task, it is highly unlikely that the human programmer of the robot could have anticipated the existence of this particular object, and even if this were the case, it is unlikely that the programmer could have anticipated its use as a container, and provided a parameter to measure the amount of liquid it might contain.

This second goal of formalizing and automating the "problem setup" phase of reasoning about physical systems does not explicitly require a qualitative formulation of the underlying physical laws, nor does it necessarily impose any particular solution techniques. However, the distinctions made by qualitative formulations are precisely those needed to make the decisions needed for steps 2, segmentation, and 3, model construction. So we see that attempts to directly apply classical physics, such as the programs Newton [dK77] and Mecho [Bun78], to automated reasoning about dynamic physical situations generally rely on an initial qualitative analysis to guide application of physical laws. Mecho is a particularly interesting example of this paradigm.

The initial focus of Mecho research was static situation analysis. For this task, Mecho addresses the model formulation and transformation steps of the overall problem solving model we have presented. Mecho starts with an initial situation description, elaborates it with stored subsituation descriptions whose preconditions are satisfied, and then formulates a mathematical model of the elaborated situation based on a domain theory. It then applies the mathematical problem solving capabilities of Press to solve the resulting system of equations. This technique was quite successful in analyzing such static problems. However, an attempt to apply Mecho to the problem of prediction in dynamic situations [Bun78] revealed the desirability of preceding the detailed quantitative analysis with a qualitative analysis in order to gather additional information needed in the model formulation step of the quantitative analysis.

The solution techniques to be applied in step 4 should be separated from other aspects of qualitative physics. Most work in qualitative physics has used constraint-satisfaction techniques to perform a global search for consistent solutions to sets of qualitative relationships between variables. This is a qualitative analog of numerical analysis. Classical physics has tended to prefer the derivation of closed-form solutions where possible, and Bundy has shown in the Press system [BW81] that this technique can be automated quite successfully for the analysis of physical systems. Kuipers [Kui84] has shown the power of using rewrite techniques for analyzing qualitative systems as well, but symbolic manipulation of a set of qualitative functional relationships has probably not received as much attention among the qualitative physics community as it deserves. Recently, however, Sacks [Sac85] has developed a system for qualitative mathematical reasoning based on symbolic manipulation of qualitative mathematical descriptions of a physical situation.

3.1 Uses of QP Theory

Consider the potential uses of a qualitative physical theory:

1. Determining what is happening in a dynamic physical situation. That is, given a description of some of the objects in a situation and observations of some of the parameters of those objects, deduce what other objects must exist and what processes are active.

2. Predicting what will happen in some future situation. Again, given a partial description of a situation, determine how that situation will evolve in terms of disappearance of existing objects, introduction of new objects, or changes in the set of processes that are active.

3. Determining how a situation may have come about (although this is very hard, in general, since it may require postulating the prior existence of objects no longer in evidence).

4. Checking for consistency, planning experiments, explaning, and performing a variety of other tasks.

Many of these tasks are constructive in nature. That is, an automated reasoner would not start with a complete and consistent description of the physical system to be reasoned about, but has only a partial description. It must then supplement this partial description with internal knowledge known to be applicable to situations of the kind being analyzed. The claim that the reasoning tasks are constructive implies that the internal knowledge the system has does not describe the target physical system in its entirety, but rather applies to individual elements of that system. Forbus deduces from this a requirement that a useful theory must consist of *composable* elements. That is, the elements of the theory must be such that they can be composed to build descriptions of larger systems, and that the deductions sanctioned by it must then reach correct conclusions when applied to these composite descriptions.

But QP theory is not just about physical systems in general; it is specifically about dynamics. Dynamics is about change, and therefore a useful theory of dynamics must describe how change occurs. Forbus identifies two components of descriptions of change. First, the theory must provide a means of describing the direct effects of some cause of change (e.g., if I apply a force to the end of a lever, it will move). Second, the theory must provide a means of describing ways in which these effects can be propagated through the physical system to cause yet other effects (e.g., if the lever I pushed is connected to a second lever, the second lever may also move).

3.2 Process versus Device-Centered Theories

The central thesis of QP theory is that all change in a physical system is the result of active processes and that these processes should be explicitly represented and reasoned about. These processes, together with contingent descriptions of partial composite situations, called *individual-views*, are the composable elements out of which complex situation descriptions are constructed. The introduction of processes makes QP theory a *process centered*, rather than a *device centered*, theory. A device-centered theory (such as de Kleer's [dKB84b]) requires identifying all relevant components, as well as all possible interactions among these components, in advance; a process-centered one does not. In a device-centered theory, descriptions of change are distributed among the objects participating in the change. An object description, therefore, must explicitly include descriptions of the way the object interacts in all change processes in which it can participate. This makes QP theory more interesting than device-centered theories for reasoning about ill-understood physical situations, and Forbus claims some evidence that human understanding of a domain tends to move from being process centered to device centered as it matures.

Also, device-centered theories cannot represent causality in the form of occurring processes. For example, consider the following example of fluid flow:

> Consider a liquid flow occurring between two tanks that are partially filled with water and connected by a pipe. In the device-centered ontology, this situation would be represented by the level in one tank rising, the level in the other tank falling, and the motion of the liquid in the pipe from source to destination. But the cause of these changes, the liquid flow, is not represented.[1]

What Forbus seems to be saying here is that the most natural causal explanation for why the level of water is dropping in one tank is that the water in that tank is flowing into the other tank. The process provides a convenient label for the complex of changes that occur together and that, as a group, constitute fluid flow.

Finally, device-centered descriptions do not provide for objects vanishing or appearing (e.g., the water in one of the containers vanishing when the container becomes "empty"), nor do they make it easy to represent effects of objects on other objects (e.g., changes in connectivity).

Forbus introduced the notion of a process in part to handle these problems. That is, the reason water is vanishing from one container and appearing in the other is that there is an active instance of a fluid-flow process. Processes also serve to delineate the boundaries of a system. If one considers all the objects in a situation and all the process instances active between various groups of these objects, then the processes can be seen to impose a partitioning on the set of objects, where each of the objects in a partition

---

[1] [For84], p. 16

interacts with at least one of the other objects in that partition through one or more active processes. Each partition corresponds to the spatial bounds for a history at that point in time. Since processes also describe how the objects will change, they also provide a mechanism for determining the temporal evolution of the objects involved. Processes, then, also serve as a way of generating histories.

3.3 Qualitative Process Theory - Definitions and Examples

QP theory identifies three fundamental components of a physical situation, the *objects* involved, the relevant *quantities* describing interesting parameters of those objects, and the *processes* that are operating on or between the objects. Objects are primitive in QP theory, and all that is known about them is contained in the predicates asserted that mention them and the quantities describing object parameter values. A second-class object, the *composite object*, is a conditionalized object, which is said to exist as long as its underlying objects exist and maintain the relationships that define the view or process that asserts its existence. For example, if there is some liquid in a container, then there is an instance of a *contained liquid*. As long as the liquid remains in the the container, then the instance of contained liquid is said to exist. Except for their contingent existence, individual composite objects are first-class objects and can appear anywhere a primitive object can.

Figure 3.1, from Forbus, shows the definition of the circumstances under which a contained liquid can be said to exist. The *Defview* form shown in the figure is used to define contingent objects or relations between objects. Literals that begin with "?" are variables. The form "(Contained-Liquid ?con ?sub)" is used to build a canonical identifier for each instance of the view that is found. After the canonical identifier, the Defview consists of four labelled sections, *Individuals*, *Preconditions*, *QuantityConditions*, and *Relations*.

The Individuals section names a list of individuals that must be found to create an instance of the view. Each individual specification starts with a variable name and then lists one or more predicates that must be true of any candidate binding for the variable. The Preconditions and QuantityConditions sections list a series of relations that must be true in order for the view instance to be active. The difference between the two sections is that the predicates and relations that are not changed within the theory are listed in Preconditions, whereas those that may change are listed under QuantityConditions. This is simply for implementation efficiency: Preconditions can be considered as constants during some deductions. In the form

((A (amount-of-in ?sub ?con)) Greater-than 0)

(amount-of-in ?sub ?con) is a ***quantity***. Quantities in QP theory have two numbers, an ***amount***, and a ***derivative*** (with respect to time). The (A <quantity>) form extracts the amount aspect of the quantity. The condition above, then, simply states that there must be some nonzero amount of the candidate liquid within the container for this view to apply. Finally, the Relations section lists a set of predicates and relations that are true when all conditions for the view instance are met. The ***Introduces-uniquely*** form, for example, establishes an if-and-only-if inference between satisfaction of all conditions for the view instance (Forbus says the view instance is ***active*** when this is the case), and an existence predicate on the named composite object. The other relation asserted by the contained-liquid view is that of a qualitative equality ($Q =$) between the amount of the contained liquid and the amount of liquid in the container.

```
(Defview (Contained-Liquid ?con ?sub)
    :Individuals
        ((?con (container ?con))
         (?sub (substance ?sub)
               (= (state ?sub) liquid)))
    :Preconditions
        ((Can-Contain-Substance ?con ?sub))
    :QuantityConditions
        ((A (amount-of-in ?sub ?con)) > 0)
    :Relations
        (Introduces-uniquely (c-1 ?con ?sub))
        ((amount-of (c-1 ?con ?sub))
         Q= (amount-of-in ?sub ?con))))
```

FIGURE 3.1. Contained-Liquid View

Many of the effects of processes on objects can be modeled by changing the parameters of the objects, that is, properties whose values are drawn from a continuous range. The representation for an object parameter in QP theory is a ***quantity***. As mentioned above, a quantity in QP theory is associated with two numbers, its amount and its derivative. Actually, each quantity is represented in QP theory by four components:

1. The *magnitude* of the amount of the quantity.
2. The *sign* of the amount.
3. The *magnitude* of the derivative.
4. The *sign* of the derivative.

A sign is a discrete, three-valued attribute with possible values $\{-\,0\,+\}$. The value of an amount in a situation is also represented in a *quantity space*.[2] The quantity space for a number consists of all the amounts to which it is potentially related in the situation being modeled. Zero is always included in every quantity space and relates the quantity space representation with sign information. For example, the sign of a number is minus exactly when its value is less than zero. Forbus claims this representation is one of very few qualitative representation schemes that does not violate his "relevance" principle:[3]

> ...qualitative reasoning about something continuous requires some kind of quantization to form a discrete set of symbols; the distinctions made by the quantization must be relevant to the kinds of reasoning being performed.

Although it is true that the distinctions made by the quantization (and the associated partial order) are relevant to the kinds of reasoning being performed, they are not always sufficient with respect to that reasoning, nor are they necessarily complete with respect to the tasks for which the reasoning is being performed. Again, this is discussed further in Chapter 4.

Quantities are related to one another through *relations*, which can be either ordering relations, functional relationships, or influences. Influences can only occur within processes and will be discussed in that context. Ordering relations include simple statements regarding the relative values of amount or derivative aspects of quantities, such as

```
((A (level p)) Equal-to (A (level q)))
((A (pressure p)) Greater-than 0)
```

Functional relations are a qualitative analog of normal mathematical functions whose domain and range are real numbers, with the restriction that functional relations must be monotonic. Nonmonotonic relations are

[2] Note that there is some terminological confusion here. Despite the fact that it is called a "quantity" space, it is actually a representation for only one aspect of a quantity, the magnitude of its amount. But the derivative of one quantity can be the amount of another, so derivatives can also be represented in quantity spaces. The quantity representation used in QP theory is discussed further in Chapter 4.

[3] From Forbus [For84].

handled by separating them into piecewise monotonic regions and expressing each region separately. Actually, functional dependence, rather than strict functionality, is expressed in QP theory. That is, a functional relationship statement does not exclude the possibility of dependence of the range variable on other quantities not named in the functional relationship. Functional relationships can be named, permitting the propagation of ordering information through separate instances of the same named relationship. Also, the functional relationship can be supplemented with individual point mappings. Again from Forbus:

```
(Function-Spec pressure-function
               (pressure ?self) Q+ (level ?self)))
               (Correspondence ((A (level ?self))
               (A ((height bottom) ?container))
               ((A (pressure ?self))
               0))
```

The first predicate above, the *function-spec*, specifies that the pressure of a fluid (at the bottom of a container) is qualitatively proportional to the level of the fluid within the container, and that the functional form is identical for all instances (i.e., for all $Q+$ relations also surrounded by a "pressure-function" function-spec). This function specification permits the inference that two containers with the same fluid level have the same bottom pressure.[4] The second, the *correspondence*, specifies that the pressure is zero when the level of the fluid is at the bottom of the container.

The final fundamental component in QP theory models is the *process*. A process is the mechanism of change in QP theory. Examples of processes in QP theory include fluid flow and linear motion. A process acts to change a situation by influencing some parameter(s) of objects in the situation. Since a fundamental assumption of QP theory is that instances of active processes must be discovered (i.e., they are not specified as part of the initial situation description), more than one process may be influencing the same parameter. An algorithm known as influence resolution is used to determine the actual effect of the combination of processes acting on a parameter. As can be seen in Fig. 3.2, a process looks exactly like an individual view, with the addition of the *Influences* section. The (Local ...) form in the Relations section declares a local parameter that is instantiated for each instance of the process. The first form in the influences section states that the derivative of the heat of the destination is qualitatively proportional to the flow rate of the heat flow. That is, the amount of heat gained by the destination per unit time is greater for higher heat-flow rates. The second form shows the other possible relation which can appear in the influences

[4] Actually, this should also include fluid density.

section, the $I-$. In this case, it states that the rate at which heat is lost by the source is qualitatively proportional to the heat flow rate. Again, remember that like $Q+$ and $Q-$, these are *partial* specifications of the underlying functional relationships and hold only in the absence of other conflicting influences.

```
(DefProcess (Heat-flow ?src ?dst ?path)
    :Individuals
        ((?src (Physobj ?src) (Has-value ?src heat))
         (?dst (Physobj ?dst) (Have-Value ?dst heat))
         (?path (Heat-Path ?path)
                (Heat-Connection ?path ?src ?dst)))
    :Preconditions
        (Heat-Aligned ?path)
    :QuantityConditions
        ((A (temp ?src)) Greater-than (A (temp ?dst)))
    :Relations
        ((Local flow-rate (Quantity flow-rate))
         (flow-rate Q= (- (temp ?src) (temp ?dst)))
         ((A flow-rate) Greater-than 0))
    :Influences
        (((heat ?dst) I+ flow-rate)
         ((heat ?dst) I- flow-rate))))
```

FIGURE 3.2. Heat-Flow Process

3.4 Reasoning in QP Theory

Gizmo, Forbus' first implementation of QP theory, combines this basic information with an initial system description to perform measurement interpretation and envisioning. Four basic deductions are combined to perform these two tasks. The four are *elaboration*, *determination of process and view structure*, *influence resolution*, and *limit analysis*. Each of these is described below.

The first deduction, *elaboration*, is a process in which all possible view and process instances that might occur in a situation are added to it. This involves finding all possible groups of individuals that can match the individuals needed for each process or view and that do or could possibly meet the conditions and preconditions. Since active processes and views can introduce new objects into a state, this procedure must then recognize the possibility that each new possible process or view instance might enable yet other process or view instances. The possible computational complexity of this matching process is reduced by distinguishing between *logical* and *physical* existence. An object is said to logically exist in a situation if we either know it to exist or have identified some possible process or view instance that, if active, could cause it to exist. Physical existence is the assertion that a view or process is active in a particular state of the system under consideration, or that a contingent object actually exists in that state. For example, if there are two containers of liquid connected by a pipe, then it is logically possible that a fluid-flow process may be active between the containers. Physical existence of the fluid flow during some particular time interval, however, will depend on the amount of liquid in the containers, whether or not any valves in the pipe are open, and so on.

By adding all possible logically existing objects to a situation simultaneously, elaboration can be completed in one pass, without asserting the possibly inconsistent statement that all of these objects actually do exist simultaneously in some actual state of the physical system being analyzed. Elaboration will terminate when a partial order can be established among views and processes that introduce new objects into the situation, where the basic ordering predicate is that view or process definition "A" introduces an object that view or process definition "B" can match as an individual to create a new instance. It is the responsibility of the theory builder to ensure that this condition is met.

The second basic deduction is the *determination of view and process structures*, that is, selecting from the above determined set of all possible view and process instances those subsets that are mutually consistent, as well as consistent with the known facts about the situation, and that are interrelated. If we consider the two-container example mentioned earlier, two possible processes are one involving a fluid flow from the first container to the second and one involving a fluid flow from the second container to the first. However, although these two processes are both logically possible, they cannot occur simultaneously, since they require contradictory quantity conditions (flow from container one to container two requires that the level in container one be higher than the level in container two, and vice versa). Starting with any process or view instance, then, we can grow a set by adding to it each process or view instance which requires conditions and individuals consistent with the existing set, and which involves at least one object referenced by at least one process or view in the set. The sets identified by this procedure are *p-components*, groups of processes and views that can be considered independently and that serve as a basis for generating histories. Processes, then, provide a means for determining how the world can be carved up into individual chunks of space-time (histories). The set of p-components that reference overlapping sets of objects are partial descriptions of the possible states of the system comprising those objects.

The third deduction is *influence resolution*, a process in which the set of influences on each situation parameter (determined in the previous step) is resolved to determine the actual effect of the situation on each parameter. Several factors affect the ability of QP theory to perform this resolution. First, Forbus states that no loops are permitted in QP theory. That is, if one parameter is qualitatively proportional to a second, then the second cannot be qualitatively proportional to the first. Also, influences (i.e., direct causes of change: $I+/I-$) are assumed to carry much more information than qualitative proportionalities (passive propagators of change). Although Forbus assumes that influences are additive, he does not make this assumption for qprops. This means that conflicting influences can be resolved if magnitude information is available, whereas conflicting qprops cannot be so resolved. Finally, Gizmo does not permit a parameter to be both directly (via $I+/I-$) and indirectly (via $Q+/Q-$) influenced simultaneously. One result of all this is a clear notion of causality extractable from the influence diagram for any state of a system. It is not clear, however, how we can enforce these requirements given a theory consisting of multiple, separate entity, view, and process models that can interact in unanticipated combinations.

Another point of view on the problems that can occur in influence resolution is that, when a view and process structure corresponds to a single possible state of the situation being analyzed, then influence resolution will be able to assign unique values to all parameters. However, when a view and process structure can correspond to more than one state, influence resolution will only be able to assign values to those parameters that have the same value in all states. We use the term "state" here to mean a complete and unique assignment of values to all parameters in the situation. When the distinction between view and process structure and the corresponding state(s) is irrelevant, we will use the terms interchangeably.

Finally, *limit analysis* is a deduction in which predictions are made regarding possible transitions out of each possible view and process structure. The transitions identified are changes in the process and view structures of the situation. These can be identified as follows. First, deduction 2, determination of view and process structure, when identifying a possible set of process and view instances, builds a quantity space for each parameter in the situation reflecting the ordering relations that must hold for the included processes and views to be active or inactive. Second, influence resolution determines how each parameter is changing. limit analysis combines these two sources of information to determine the processes whose status will change first, as a result of changes in orderings in parameter quantity spaces, resulting in a transition to a qualitatively different state.

Ambiguity can occur here when lack of information prevents determination either of which of several possible transitions will occur first or in which direction a parameter is changing.

3.5 Historical Background

In the *Naive Physics Manifesto* [Hay79b], Hayes called for the construction of large-scale formalizations of our common-sense knowledge about the physical world. In this call, Hayes protested that most prior work in AI on reasoning about physical systems dealt only with artificially small toy domains, and that the techniques developed for these toy domains, in general, did not scale up to the needs of more comprehensive theories. He also stressed the need to be concerned more with the content of these formalizations and less with the syntactic details of representation. He outlined an approach to the problem, namely, that of identifying and developing theories for "clusters" of tightly connected concepts. Implicit in the work on QP theory is the belief that various kinds of dynamics are examples of such clusters.

QP theory apparently grew out of an attempt by Forbus to implement a reasoner based on Hayes' *Naive Ontology for Liquids* [Hay79a]. Hayes presented ***histories*** as an alternative to situations and as a solution to the frame problem [Hay71]. In situational calculus [FN71], situations are used to model the world at different times. Each situation describes the complete world state at an instant of time. The frame problem arises in the determination of those facts that carry forward from one situation to the next. Since a situation is spatially unbounded, we have no way of determining whether or not any causes of change, in addition to those explicitly stated, are active. Therefore, we cannot invoke any kind of inertia[5] or closed-world[6] principle. While a situation is temporally bounded, but spatially unbounded, a history is a piece of space-time with both spatial and temporal boundaries. These boundaries are determined by causality, and therefore one can safely assume that external causes have no effect within a history. Hayes further assumes that all active causes within a history are known. We can now invoke closed-world and inertia assumptions, thereby solving the frame problem. The use of histories introduces two new problems, however: determining the spatial bounds of a history and determining whether history intersections correspond to interactions between physical

[5] An inertia principle is one that states that any predicate or relation that is true in situation s1 is true in the situation following s1, unless explicitly referred to in the axioms describing the event that transforms s1 into its successor.

[6] A closed-world principle states that there are no causes of change active other than those explicitly noted - probably invalid for a spatially unbounded description!

components of the respective histories. Forbus [For84] points out that, although histories are an adequate descriptive device, Hayes provides no way to generate them out of more primitive system descriptions.

Another major contribution of Hayes' work on naive physics was the recognition of the important role of context-dependent individuation in reasoning about the world [Hay79a]. For example, the first drop of water entering a cup creates a new object: a contained liquid within the cup. Subsequent drops do not create additional objects but simply increase the *amount* of the contained-liquid object. Although it might seem that this could be accomplished more simply by providing a model of a cup with an "amount of contained liquid" parameter, initialized to zero, this solution fails for at least two reasons. First, it presumes that we can identify in advance every object in a situation that might potentially act as a container, including those accidently assembled during the course of evolution of the situation. Second, it provides no way of modeling a situation in which two immiscible liquids both exist in the same container. This form of reasoning, although it simplifies the formalization of much common-sense knowledge, requires that any system using such formalizations be able to reason about the appearance and disappearance of such contingent objects.

Finally, Hayes claimed a special role for "taxonomic" reasoning, or reasoning by exclusion, in naive physics. He applied this form of reasoning determining the events occurring in a situation. First, he would determine that some class of event was occurring; then, reasoning by exclusion over all the events in that class, he would determine which element of the class was the relevant one. Although Forbus does not directly use this technique at the level of possible occurring events, he does rely heavily on the basic technique of propositional reasoning by exclusion over "taxonomic" or one-of sets of propositions regarding variable values and object or process states.

Whereas Hayes' work provides the formal background for QP theory, much of its pragmatics have been influenced by the work of Stallman, Sussman, and Steele. In early work on ARS and EL [SS77], Stallman and Sussman explored the use of constraint propagation and dependency-directed backtracking as fundamental techniques for reasoning about physical systems. De Kleer [dK79] [dKB84b], building on this work, demonstrated the utility of these same techniques with qualitative quantity representations. Like Stallman and Sussman, de Kleer continued to use a device-centered ontology in his description of physical systems. This involved representing a system as a fixed set of components, interconnected in a fixed manner, and therefore required the identification of all possible interactions in advance. Forbus noted, however, that this makes it difficult to represent and reason about situations in which the objects themselves change (e.g., a kettle full of boiling water, in which the water eventually all boils off).

De Kleer also laid the foundation for the QP theory representation of quantities in his work on incremental qualitative (IQ) analysis [dK79]. In this work, he identified the sign of the derivative as a crucial qualitative abstraction in reasoning about change. He demonstrated the ability to deduce, for example, that water in a kettle on the stove will heat up when the stove is on. However, as Forbus observed, it is not possible, using only the sign of the derivative, to deduce that the water will eventually boil, because there is no way to represent the static limit conditions at which processes start or stop. Forbus extends the sign abstraction using a partial ordering of related quantities, which he terms a *quantity space*. This notion has been described in detail in a preceding section of this chapter.

3.6 Summary

In this chapter we reviewed qualitative process (QP) theory, starting with the need for a qualitative theory of physical reasoning and some of the requirements potential uses impose on such a theory, including composability and effect propagation mechanisms. We then reviewed in detail the representation and inference elements of QP theory, emphasizing the notions of objects, parameters, and processes. Finally, we reviewed some of the historical background in which the development of QP theory took place. Further detail on QP theory can be found in [For84].

4

Application of QP Theory to Process Control - An Example

We now present an extended example, a model of a furnace for a continuous-flow chemical process. Figure 4.1 shows a simplified chemical furnace in which reactants in particulate form enter from the left-hand top port and react when heated to the proper temperature within the furnace. The product collects in the bottom of the furnace, and an off-gas is produced as a by-product, which exits out the top right port. We can imagine for the moment that this is a batch process, and, when the furnace is full of product, it is shut down and emptied by a process not shown here. We are interested in control of industrial processes like this; in particular, we would like to determine what kinds of things might be happening in this situation and the response the furnace would make to various control actions we might take.

Classical control theory has long studied at least the latter of these two issues and formulates models of such situations in terms of quantitative, often differential, equations relating variables in the situation. A quantitative approach is often inapplicable, however, for at least two reasons. First, the data regarding furnace parameters are uncertain and incomplete. Sensors are not available for measuring many of the needed parameters, and when they are available, the cost of installation and/or maintenance can be prohibitive. Second, the necessary quantitative models for various furnace processes are frequently unknown. Even if they were known, we would still need a preliminary qualitative reasoning step to determine which processes were active and which process models were applicable.

QP theory, on the other hand, seems to offer the possibility of defining a qualitative vocabulary similar to that used by experienced chemical plant personnel when talking about such processes, and it provides inference procedures that offer the potential of producing similar conclusions to those produced by such personnel. Returning to the example, upon examination we recognize several objects. There is a container (the furnace), some product in the furnace, some reactants above the product, and a heat source. Figure 4.2 shows the situation definition form used in QP theory to provide the initial description of the example reaction system.

In addition to knowing about the objects involved, one needs to know several facts about how these objects can change. For example, when a heat source is near an object that can be heated, and the orientation of the

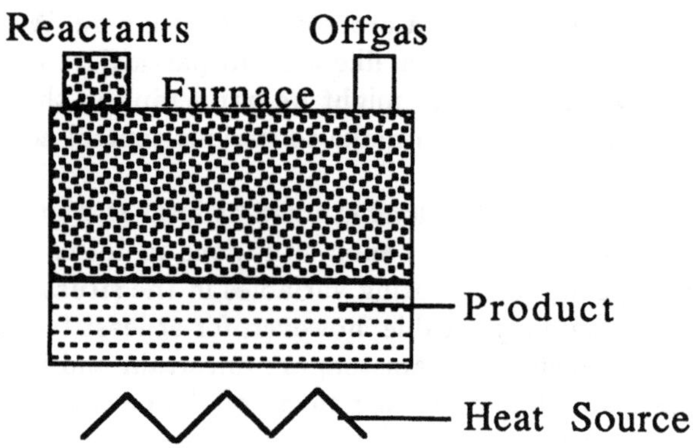

FIGURE 4.1. A Simplified Chemical Furnace

```
(defscenario refinery
  :Individuals (
    (c-s product furnace) (c-s reactants furnace)
    (c-s reactants bin) off-gas-path (c-s off-gas furnace)
    furnace heater heat-conduction-path bin offtake
    reactant-path (heat-path furnace))
  :Facts (
    (container furnace) (container bin) (container offtake)
    (substance reactants) (substance product)
    (substance off-gas) (chemical-furnace furnace)
    (product (c-s product furnace)) (heat-source heater)
    (heat-path heat-conduction-path)
    (heat-path (heat-path furnace))
    (heat-connection heat-conduction-path heater
                     (c-s product furnace))
    (flow-path reactant-path) (flow-path off-gas-path)
    (Material-flow-connection reactant-path bin furnace)
    (Material-flow-connection off-gas-path furnace offtake))
  :Always (
    (Heat-connection heat-conduction-path heater
                     (c-s product furnace))
    (Heat-connection (heat-path furnace)
                     off-gas-path reactant-path)
    ((A (temp heater)) Greater-than
                       (A (reaction-temp reactants))))
  :In-Situation (T0
    ((A (pressure (c-s reactants bin))) Greater-than
     (A (pressure (c-s reactants furnace))))
    ((A (Temp heater)) Greater-than
                       (A (Temp (c-s product furnace))))
    ((A (Temp (c-s product furnace))) Greater-than
     (A (reaction-temp reactants)))
    ((A (Temp (c-s reactants bin))) Less-than
     (A (Temp (c-s off-gas furnace))))
    ((A (amount-of (c-s reactants furnace))) greater-than
                                              Zero)
    ((A (amount-of (c-s reactants bin))) greater-than Zero)
    ((A (amount-of (c-s product furnace))) greater-than Zero)
    ((A (amount-of-in off-gas furnace)) Greater-than Zero)))
```

FIGURE 4.2. Chemical Furnace Initial Situation Description

two is such that heat can flow from the heat source to the object,[1] heat will flow, and the object will be heated. Also, as described earlier, a state change occurs when the reactants are heated beyond a certain point, and the reactants are converted into product plus a gas called "off-gas." Finally, there is an important heat-transfer process that takes place between the exiting off-gas and the incoming reactants.

Each of these causes of change is represented as a process in QP theory. Two of the most important and complex are shown in Figs. 4.3 and 4.4. Figure 4.3 shows the definition of the basic chemical reaction. Figure 4.4 shows a description of the countercurrent heat flow. But notice also that there is something special about the reactant, product, and off-gas objects in this situation. The individual involved is all of the substance within the furnace. If the amount were to be zero, the individual would cease to exist, but if we add more reactant to the furnace, this does not create a new individual; it simply increases the amount of an already existing individual. The view shown in Fig. 4.5 describes the conditions under which such a contained-substance individual can be said to exist and is taken directly from Forbus.

4.1 The Reaction Process

This process describes the basic state change that takes place during the reaction within the furnace. This description presumes some simpler descriptions, including the description of countercurrent heat flow presented in Fig. 4.4. Other descriptions can be found in [For84]. Several simplifications have been made to in order to reduce the complexity of the description. For example, we use a pressure model to motivate both of the material flows in and out of the furnace, rather than the more complex gravity and spatial reasoning arguments needed to model the reactant's flow accurately. A more complete description of the situation would require modelling it from the collection-of-particles perspective, as well as from the contained-substance perspective, and combining results from both views. Currently, several unsolved problems make this approach impossible.[2]

The description in Fig. 4.3 states that, when the temperature is correct,

---

[1] *Heat-path*, used by Forbus to represent this condition in his model of heat flow, is a stub at the interface between the naive fluid dynamics theory in Forbus' model and other theories not yet elaborated, such as those for spatial orientation and the actions of external agents. For example, if in a heat-flow situation the source and target are misaligned, or if there is an insulator placed between them by an external agent, then no heat will flow.

[2] The major problems here currently are the formulation of domain theories for heat transfer at the collection of particles granularity, and mechanisms for information passing between granularity levels.

fluid flows of reactants into the furnace and off-gas out of the furnace are initiated, and a heat transfer starts between the two fluid flows. Also, the amount of reactants in the furnace is influenced in a negative direction by the reaction process generation rate.

4.2 Countercurrent Heat Flow

This view describes the effects of the countercurrent heat flow between the exiting off-gas and the incoming product. An accurate model of countercurrent heat flow requires reasoning from both the contained-substance and the collection-of-molecules viewpoints, as noted by Forbus. This simplified model, however, is adequate for the purposes of this exposition. Note that it is a view, not a process. On the contained-substance level, what is described is not a change, but simply a static equilibrium condition. If this were modeled at the collection-of-molecules level of granularity, then countercurrent heat flow would be one or more processes. In such a model, countercurrent heat flow would be modeled as a cause of change in the amount of heat of individual particles as they moved through the heat-transfer zone.

The difference between a view and a process is that a view cannot contain any direct influences. A view can, however, provide a propagation path for already established influences, and that is the purpose of qualitative proportionalities. Specifically,

```
((Temp\, ?dst-flow-dst-cs)\, Q+\, (Temp\, ?dst-flow-origin-cs))
```

specifies that if the entry temperature of the reactants is increasing, then, in the absence of other indirect influences, the exit temperature is also increasing. Notice that one of the aspects of the situation we lose by modeling it at such a coarse level of granularity is the notion of a delay between change in the temperature at entry and the resulting exit temperature change. At the contained-substance level we can only capture equilibrium descriptions.

4.3 Basic Deductions

As mentioned earlier, Forbus describes four basic deductions in QP theory. More complex reasoning, such as measurement interpretation or envisioning, is built out of these basic deductions. We now review these deductions and summarize the results of applying them to our example. The results shown were obtained by program analysis of the reaction furnace example. Chapters 9 and 10 describe the algorithms used in detail, and also contain listing of the actual program output.

```
(defProcess (Reaction ?furnace ?reactants ?product ?phf)
  :Individuals (
    (?furnace (chemical-furnace ?furnace))
    (?reactants (contained-substance ?reactants)
(= reactants (substance ?reactants))
(contains ?furnace ?reactants))
    (?product (= product (substance ?product))
              (contains ?furnace ?product))
    (?phf ((process-instance heat-flow) ?phf)
          (= ?product (dst ?phf))))
  :Conditions (
    (Status ?phf Active)
    ((A (Temp ?product)) greater-than
     (A (reaction-temp reactants))))
  :Relations (
    (Introduces (c-s off-gas ?furnace))
    ((Temp (c-s off-gas ?furnace)) Q= (Temp ?product))
    (Local g-rate (Quantity g-rate))
    ((A g-rate) Greater-than Zero)
    (g-rate Q+ (Temp ?product))
    (g-rate Q+ (Temp ?reactants))
    (Introduces-uniquely (heat-path ?furnace))
    ((heat-transfer-quality (heat-path ?furnace)) Q+
     (quality ?reactants)))
  :Influences (
    ((heat ?product) I+ (flow-rate ?phf))
    ((heat ?product) I- g-rate)
    ((amount-of (c-s off-gas ?furnace)) I+ g-rate)
    ((amount-of ?product) I+ g-rate)
    ((amount-of ?reactants) I- g-rate)))
```

FIGURE 4.3. The Reaction Process

```
(defView (Countercurrent-heat-flow
   ?src ?dst ?path ?src-flow-origin-cs ?src-flow-dst-cs
   ?dst-flow-origin-cs ?dst-flow-dst-cs)
  :Individuals (
    (?src ((process-instance material-flow) ?src)
          (= ?src-flow-origin (src ?src))
  (= ?src-flow-origin-cs (material ?src))
  (= ?src-flow-dst (dst ?src))
  (= ?src-path (path ?src)))
    (?dst ((process-instance material-flow) ?dst)
          (= ?dst-flow-origin (src ?dst))
  (= ?dst-flow-origin-cs (material ?dst))
  (= ?dst-flow-dst (dst ?dst))
  (= ?dst-path (path ?dst)))
  :Conditions (
    ((A (Flow-rate ?src)) Greater-than Zero)
    ((A (Flow-Rate ?dst)) Greater-than Zero)
    ((A (Temp ?src-flow-origin-cs))
     Greater-than (A (Temp ?dst-flow-origin-cs))))
  :Relations (
    ((A (Temp src-flow-dst-cs)) Greater-than
     (A (Temp ?dst-flow-origin-cs)))
    (local Temp-lost (Quantity Temp-Lost))
    ((A Temp-lost) Greater-than Zero)
    (Temp-lost Q- (flow-rate ?src))
    (Temp-lost Q+ (Temp ?src-flow-origin-cs))
    (Temp-lost Q- (Temp ?dst-flow-origin-cs))
    ((Temp ?src-flow-dst-cs) Q- Temp-lost)
    ((Temp  ?src-flow-dst-cs) Q+  (Temp ?dst-flow-origin-cs))
    (local Temp-gained (Quantity Temp-gained))
    ((A Temp-gained) Greater-than Zero)
    (Temp-gained Q- (flow-rate ?dst))
    (Temp-gained Q+ (Temp ?src-flow-origin-cs))
    (Temp-gained Q- (Temp ?dst-flow-origin-cs))
    ((Temp ?dst-flow-dst-cs) Q+ Temp-gained)
    ((Temp ?dst-flow-dst-cs) Q+
                              (Temp ?dst-flow-origin-cs))))
```

FIGURE 4.4. Countercurrent Heat Flow

```
(DefView Contained-Liquid
    Individuals:
        ?con a container
        ?sub a substance
    Preconditions:
        Can-Contain-Substance( ?con, ?sub)
    QuantityConditions:
        Amount-of-in( ?sub, ?con) > Zero
    Relations:
        There is ?p a Piece-of-Stuff
        Amount-of( ?p) = Amount-of-in( ?Sub, ?Con)
        Made-of( ?p) = ?sub
        Container( ?p) = ?con
)
```

FIGURE 4.5. Definition of Contained Substances

1. **Elaboration** - Elaboration involves finding all possible ways in which all known view and process descriptions can match the known set of objects, using the Individuals and Conditions sections of process and view descriptions. An active view or process can introduce new objects into the situation (e.g., the reaction process, when active, introduces off-gas into the furnace), so "recursive" matching is necessary. This is simplified by matching against logically existing objects instead of physically existing ones. Applying this deduction to our situation description, given a process vocabulary that includes the reaction, heat-flow, and material fluid-flow processes and the countercurrent heat-flow view previously described, yields a set of five potential view or process instances. There can be one instance of heat flow (between the heat source and the product), one instance of the reaction process, one instance of countercurrent heat flow, and two instances of material fluid flow.

2. **Determination of View and Process Structure** - Some possible processes may have mutually contradictory enabling conditions. In this step consistent sets of active processes are determined. These consistent sets are made maximal in correspondence with an understanding of the physical world in which any process that *can* be active *is* active. Each such set describes a logically possible state of the situation. For our example, four such states exist. First, there can be a state in which no process is active. Second, there can be a state in

which only the heat flow between the heat source and the product is active. Third, all five processes can be active simultaneously. Fourth, all processes except for the heat flow can be active. In subsequent discussions we ignore the first state. The other states are referred to in the order in which they are described here (i.e., state 2, 3 or 4).

3. **Influence Resolution** - Once a maximal process set has been determined, then by the sole mechanism assumption (active processes are the only cause of change) we know all the causes of change in the corresponding state. Propagation of changes caused by direct influences from active processes, through indirect influences described in processes, views, and object descriptions, allows determination of the changes taking place in the situation (through influence resolution). Considering as an example the temperature of the product in the furnace, we determine by applying the algorithms of deduction 3 that the sign of the derivative is positive in state 2, unknown in state 3, and negative in state 4.

4. **Limit Analysis** - Many of the active process and view instances in each state are dependent on quantity ordering assumptions. Once the changes taking place have been identified, these can be compared with the quantity conditions for the state to determine the ways in which the state might end. These quantity conditions are established by recording the conditions for each process or view instance active or inactive in the state. For example, state 2 identified above will end with the temperature of the product reaching the reaction temperature of the reactants, at which point a transition to state 3 will occur. Similarly, state 4 will end with the temperature of the product dropping below the reaction temperature of the reactants, at which time a transition to state 1 (no process activity) will occur. State 3 is more problematical, since we have not been able to determine how the temperature of the product is changing. If it is increasing or stable, then state 3 continues indefinitely. However, if it is decreasing, then state 3 will eventually end with a transition to state 2. This would be followed by a transition to state 3, indicating a kind of oscillation around a stable equilibrium. Since this oscillation takes place instantaneously (because it involves transitions to and from equality - see Forbus), it is not a true oscillation, but an artifact of the situation description known as "stutter."

The basic QP theory deductions identify four possible states for a situation involving a single furnace with heat source. The state of interest for our purposes is the one in which all processes are active. From this state, we can abstract the functional relationships between variables. Figure 4.6 shows the direct and indirect influence graph for the main active state of the refinery. This graph is the result of applying the first two of the four basic inferences in QP theory. Looking at this graph, we can see the relationship between QP theory and other theories of causal reasoning. Rieger's causal analysis [Rie77], for example, would start with a network such as this. This network is also similar in appearance to the cognitive maps of Axelrod [Axe76] and again is subject to the same ambiguities as his work. QP theory takes on much more of the modeling load than most other theories of causal reasoning.

Reasoning from this graph, basic deductions 3 (influence resolution) and 4 (limit analysis) seek to determine how the state described can change. The column labeled "Influence Resolution" in Fig. 4.7 shows the results of influence resolution applied to the main active state of the reaction furnace. The symbol on the left side of the slash for each variable is the quantitative value of the amount of the variable, and the symbol on the right is the value of the derivative. A "?" indicates that influence resolution was unable to determine a unique value. One such question critical for reasoning about control is the determination of how changes of the independent parameters in the state affect it. We can often answer this question from this graph using the third basic deduction of Forbus, influence resolution, and its extension, qualitative pertubation analysis (QPA). QPA uses the algorithms of the third deduction, applied not to changes introduced internally by known active processes, but to external changes applied to otherwise independent parameters of the state by an external agent. That is, it starts with user-provided nonzero derivatives for one or more independent parameters. Using this technique, we can establish, for example, that

- If we increase the heat input, the off-gas generation rate will increase (complete results for the consequences of an increase in heater temperature are shown in the column labeled "QPA (Heater)" in Fig, 4.7).

- If we increase the reactant's temperature, the off-gas temperature will increase (complete results for the consequences of an increase in the reactant's temperature are shown in the column labeled "QPA (reactants)" in Fig. 4.7).

However, there are other questions one would like to ask, questions that QP theory is unable to answer but that one might expect a human expert to be able to answer:

- If we increase the heat input a little, how much will the generation rate increase?

- If we increase the heat input, will the off-gas exit temperature increase or decrease?

Both of these questions are important for reasoning about control in this situation. Although the former question is not one that QP theory claims to

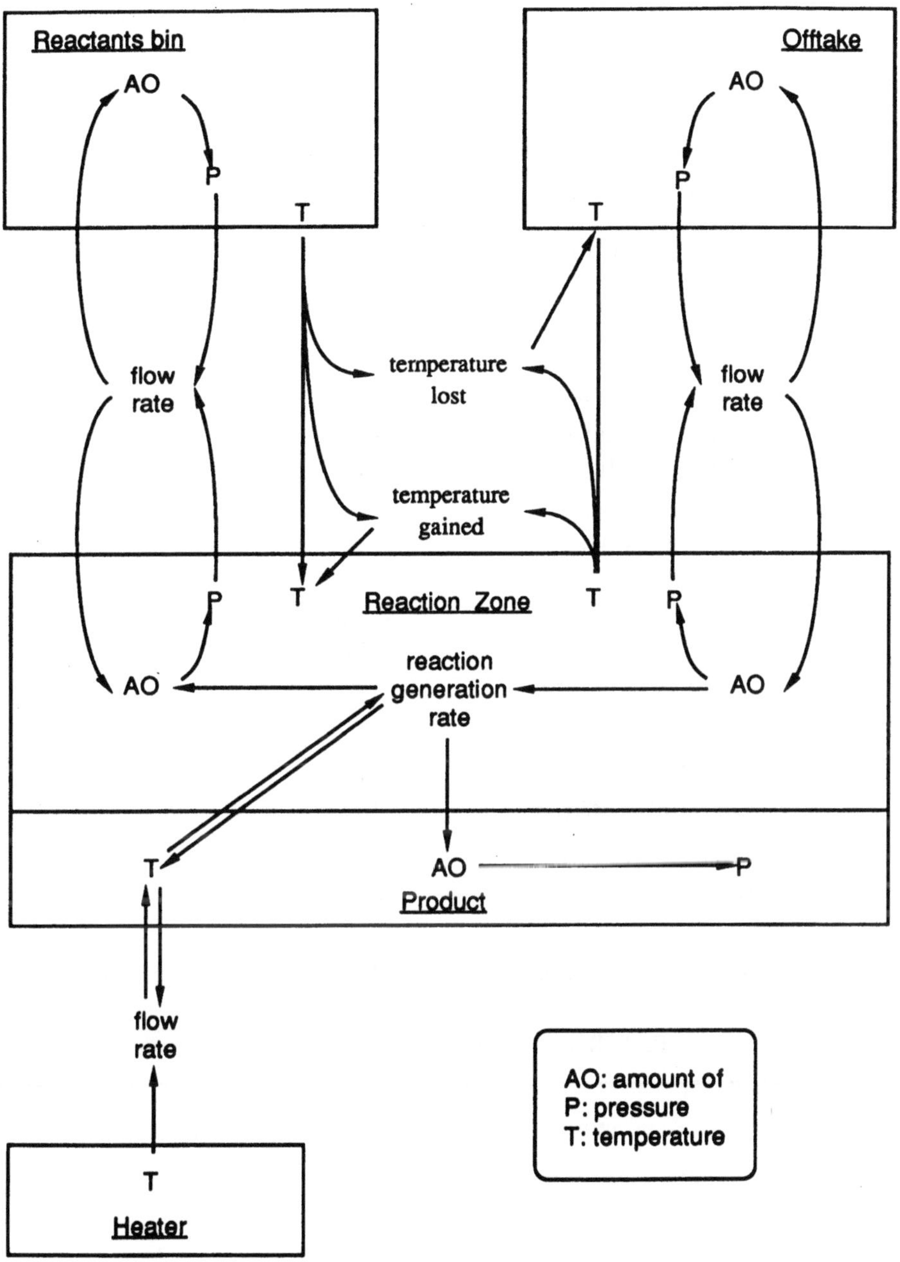

FIGURE 4.6. Influence Dependency Graph

Parameter	Influence Resolution	QPA Heater	QPA Reactant
P (reactants bin)	+/−	−	?
A (reactants bin)	+/−	−	?
T (reactants bin)	+/0	0	+
P (reactants furnace)	+/?	−	?
A (reactants furnace)	+/?	−	?
T (reactants furnace)	+/?	+	?
P (product furnace)	+/+	+	?
A (product furnace)	+/+	+	?
T (product furnace)	+/?	+	?
P (off-gas furnace)	+/?	+	?
A (off-gas furnace)	+/?	+	?
T (off-gas furnace)	+/?	+	?
P (off-gas offtake)	+/+	+	?
A (off-gas offtake)	?/+	+	?
T (off-gas offtake)	+/?	?	+
Temperature (heater)	+/0	+	0
Flow-Rate (reactants)	+/?	+	?
Flow-Rate (off-gas)	+/?	+	?
Flow-rate (heat)	+/?	+	?
G-Rate (reaction)	+/?	+	?
Temperature-Lost	+/?	?	−
Temperature-Gained	+/?	+	−

FIGURE 4.7. Results of QP Analysis of Furnace

address, the latter is directly relevant to the core of the theory and reflects a basic ambiguity in QP theory predictions about how this state might evolve. In the next chapter we identify the causes of these limitations in QP theory.

5

Ambiguity in QP Theory

We have seen that QP theory seems promising as a tool for real-time process control but is too weak in its current form. This weakness is manifested as overly qualitative answers to many of the questions that occur in reasoning about control of a physical system. In this chapter we identify the types of ambiguity that arise in basic QP theory and propose an approach to reducing this ambiguity. We do not claim that the ambiguity is a result of a failure of basic QP theory. It is precisely because its qualitative abstractions can encompass many possible more detailed descriptions that they are useful. However, the qualitative outline of a situation is often insufficient and, once obtained, must be supplemented with estimates of reduced ambiguity. Identifying such extensions, which preserve the essential character and advantages of QP theory, is the goal of this work.

This chapter begins with an analysis of the sources of ambiguity within QP theory. We identify three basic causes, all representational. These are in the representations for certainty, for parameter values, and for relationships between parameters. The chapter then continues with a brief review of some alternative representations for each of these topics. We then outline the extensions to QP theory we shall be presenting in subsequent chapters.

5.1 Ambiguity in QP Theory

We start by identifying two types of ambiguity in QP theory, *internal* and *external* ambiguity. Internal ambiguity is ambiguity at the level of abstraction of the QP description of a system, whereas external ambiguity refers to the fact that a single QP description may correspond to any of several descriptions at a more detailed level. For example, the inability to determine whether or not the container in the earlier example would explode is internal ambiguity, whereas the inability to estimate how long it might be before explosion, given that it will explode, is external ambiguity. This distinction is important for the following reason. Although it might be possible to resolve some cases of internal ambiguity by using additional information of types already defined in QP theory, or by using more powerful inference techniques, external ambiguity can only be resolved by adding new types of information, together with the appropriate inferences.

Internal ambiguity manifests itself in one of two forms. First, there is the inability to determine, given a situation description, which of several possible states a system is in (e.g., given a leaky bucket with water pouring in, is the water level rising or falling?) Second, there is the inability to determine given a specific situation, what situation will follow it. (E.g., given a closed container containing water, and a heat source heating the container, will it explode?)

External ambiguity manifests itself as the inability to determine, on a scale meaningful to an external observer, the likelihood and duration of a situation, as well as the magnitude and intrasituation evolution of the parameters of the situation. (E.g., how likely is it that the container will explode? How long before the container explodes? How fast is the water rising in the leaky bucket?)

The ambiguities described above are the result of four basic sources within QP theory:

1. The ability to represent only Boolean truth values, especially for ordering relationship assertions.

2. An inability to resolve conflicting influences.

3. An inability to order predicted state changes.

4. The lack of quantitative models of quantities, functional relationships, and time.

The first source is a limitation of the propositional logic in which QP theory is expressed. The truth value for a state is simply the conjunction of the truth values for each of the view or process status assertions in that state. These, in turn, are a conjunction of the truth values of the existence assertions on the needed individuals and the truth values of certain ordering relations between quantities. Since these truth values can only be expressed as Booleans, it is impossible to express or estimate likelihoods for states in other than Boolean terms.

The second source of ambiguity in QP theory is caused by lack of ordering or relative strength information on functional relationships between quantities. When conflicting influences impinge on a single quantity, QP theory is unable to determine the resulting direction of change for the quantity.[1] This is a major cause of both types of internal ambiguity. That is, it can result in a physically unrealizable state matching an observed situation, as well as predict some transitions out of a state that cannot, in fact, take place. De Kleer points out that such predictions are valid as long as there is *some* physical realization of the model that would produce each of the

---

[1]For example, $(A\, Q+\, B)$ and $(A\, Q-\, C)$. If both B and C have negative derivatives, there is no way to determine the sign of the derivative for A. Note that since we know nothing about the form of either of the influences, or even whether or not they are independent, information about the relative magnitudes of the derivatives does not help.

predicted behaviors. However, our concern is not with the hypothetical validity of the prediction procedure, but rather with the inexpressiveness of a modeling language that limits our ability to suitably restrict the class of systems a model covers.

The third source of ambiguity listed above is the inability to order predicted state changes. The basic source is the inability to resolve the following situation:

Given:	$(A > B), (C > D)$
	$Ds(A) = -, Ds(B) = 0, Ds(C) = -, Ds(D) = 0$
Determine:	Which ordering relationship will change first?

Since process instance activity is often conditioned on such ordering relationships, the determination of which relation changes first may affect the determination of how the current state will end (by identifying the process that will start or end first, terminating the current state). In order to resolve this situation, it is not sufficient merely to have magnitude information on the derivatives, since we cannot, in general, assume they are constant. Rather, we need three separate pieces of information:

1. Magnitude information on the values $(A - B)$ and $(C - D)$.
2. Magnitude information on the *starting* values of dA and dB.
3. Information about the shape of the derivatives over the interval between the start and end of the state. This may be derivable from information about the shape of control inputs over the interval and shape information about the partial functions influencing A and B.

We see, then, that the ambiguity of concern in QP theory is largely the result of limitations in the representations for truth values, quantities, and functional relationships. The next section briefly reviews some options for extending the QP theory representations for each of these three items.

5.2 Representation Alternatives

5.2.1 Representations for Uncertainty

There are three basic motivations for considering expanded uncertainty representation in QP theory when applied to process control. First, available measurements are often vague or unreliable. Second, there is often a priori information available about the likelihood of specific events or situations. Third, it is often important to be able to provide some estimate of the likelihood of various possible interpretations of an observation or outcomes of a prediction.

In considering this third need in particular, note that a partial ordering analogous to that used for quantities, such as that proposed by Doyle, is not sufficient. It is important for planning purposes to know not just that one event is more likely than another, but how likely the two events are in some absolute sense. Thus we are driven to consider a numeric uncertainty representation. Possibilities considered include Bayesian probabilities, possibility theory, and the Dempster/Shafer theory of evidence.

Bayesian probability theory offers a well-known and well-documented method [Che85] for combining uncertain evidence to form conclusions. It suffers, though, from several well-known limitations:

- Most pragmatic implementations require that evidence be independent.
- It requires the availability of prior probabilities for all hypotheses.
- It does not permit the expression of uncertainty about the probabilities themselves.
- It does not take advantage of all of the structure of the hypothesis space (e.g., if we have independently obtained probability estimates for three mutually exclusive hypotheses, we should be able to combine them to obtain refined estimates).

Possibility theory and reasoning systems based on it, such as approximate reasoning [Zad73], provide an attractive alternative that does not make the strong independence assumption nor require a complete set of priors. In some formulations it does permit the expression of uncertainty about the possibilities themselves. Also, partially inconsistent evidence is handled quite naturally by simply intersecting the pieces of evidence. However, because no independence assumptions are made in the most general formulation of possibility theory, the truth values for conclusions are often weaker then one might hope for. Possibility theory has been shown to be a consistent but more general framework within which Bayesian Probabilities exist as a limiting case [Zad85].

A relatively recent alternative uncertainty representation is the Dempster/Shafer theory of evidence [Sha76]. This theory, which can be seen as intermediate between probability theory and possibility theory, retains the independence assumption of probability theory, but permits representation of uncertainty of belief and provides mechanisms for combining conflicting evidence. In addition, recent work by Lowrance [LG83], Baldwin [Bal85a], Barnett[Bar81], Gordon and Shortliffe [GS85], and Yen [Yen85] has adapted this theory to various specific hypothesis space structures. We have selected an adaptation of the work by Baldwin as the underlying uncertainty mechanism used to support our extensions to QP theory. Baldwin's system, as well as our adaptation of it, is described in detail in Chapter 5.

5.2.2 Representations for Parameters of Physical Systems

In our review of QP theory, we have seen that much of the ambiguity in its conclusions is directly attributable to its method for representing continuous parameters. In this section we briefly review some options for continuous parameter representation.

One axis along which parameter representations can be sorted is the degree of expressiveness provided by the representation. Some examples along this axis are real numbers, interval values, and linguistic variables. The use of real numbers to represent the values of quantities seems natural but raises several problems. First, real numbers provide no way to represent uncertainty. That is, if we state that a temperature is 100 degrees, do we mean within 1 degree, or within 15 degrees? Second, real numbers do not combine well with a propositional fact representation. The entire result of a computation is represented as a single proposition. The propositions "(X has-value 3.0)" and "(X has-value 3.001)" are distinct, and as a result this approach does not permit easy sharing of inferences and data among alternative search paths during problem solving. This makes real numbers expensive to maintain in a propositional truth maintenance system (TMS)[2] of the sort that underlies the QP theory implementation. Finally, they fail what Forbus calls his "relevance" criterion. That is, they permit the expression of distinctions that are irrelevant to the needs of the reasoner and therefore complicate problem solving.

Interval value representations [Moo66] offer distinct advantages over the use of single-valued real numbers in cases in which parameters are not known precisely or are varying too rapidly to be accurately characterized by a single value. Unfortunately, they are subject to rapid widening of the interval as computation takes place. This is due to two causes:

1. The source of uncertainty is not tracked and as a result can be repeatedly added into the same computation, although each source should only be added once:

$$\begin{array}{rr} \text{Suppose} & A = [0,1], \text{ and } B = A \\ \text{Then} & A - B = [-1,1] \\ \text{But the real answer is} & 0!^{3} \end{array}$$

2. Also, the interval must contain all possible values, no matter how unlikely.

Finally, intervals are subject to the same criticisms as real numbers with respect to how they fit propositional fact representations and their failure of the relevance test.

---

[2] An overview of propositional truth maintenance is provided in Chapter 5.

Another important representation for numeric information is the mean/standard-deviation form. In this form, a quantity is represented by a pair of real numbers, the first the mean value and the second the standard deviation of a probability distribution for the actual value of the quantity. This representation has some attractive aspects, including reduction of the "rapid widening" problem of an interval representation. However, it, like the other continuous representations, does not provide for easy sharing of information among alternate solution paths.

Linguistic variables [Zad75a] can be seen as an extended interval representation that reduces range-widening problems due to the second contribution cited above. Specifically, although a range of possible values is specified for a variable, the *possibility* or likelihood of the variable assuming each value in the range is assigned a value from [0,1], instead of being restricted to only the individual values 0 or 1. As a result, the bounds on the result of a computation involving linguistic variables can be much tighter than the bounds of the corresponding interval computation.

The internal representation for a linguistic variable can be either continuous or discrete. A continuous internal representation is subject to the same relevance criticisms as the interval representation. A discrete internal representation, however, offers at least the potential of selecting a relevant discretization. Also, a discrete internal representation matches well with the propositional TMS.

All of the above representations are continuous, with the exception of the discrete internal representation for a linguistic variable; that is, they all allow each parameter to take an infinite number of arbitrarily closely spaced values. Alternatively, we can represent parameters discretely. Discrete representations could be numeric (e.g., integer arithmetic, discrete linguistic variables) or symbolic (e.g., LOC(Box) = 'On Table'). Forbus uses a form of symbolic discrete representation in QP theory, partial ordering of quantities, and a numeric discrete representation for one critical value, zero. He claims that these representations satisfy his relevance criterion, that is, that they make only those distinctions relevant to the reasoner.

Although it is true that the distinctions made by the partial order are *relevant* to the kinds of reasoning being performed, they are not always *complete* with respect to that reasoning, nor are they necessarily *complete* with respect to the tasks for which the reasoning is being performed. As an example of incompleteness with respect to the reasoning being performed, consider the following: If two separate parameters are both trending upward (i.e., have positive derivatives), and both are approaching some limit in their respective quantity spaces, it is impossible to express in QP theory information that would permit the determination of which parameter will reach its limit first. As an example of incompleteness with respect to the purpose of the reasoning, consider a second example. Suppose we wish to determine a feasible way of heating a kettle full of water to boiling within a few minutes. QP theory provides no clue that a stove is a much more reasonable source of heat than a match.

5.2.3 Characterizations of Functional Relationships

In this section we briefly review previously studied techniques for characterizing functional relationships between parameters of a physical situation. The review is restricted to techniques intended for qualitative representation of these relationships. For review purposes, we divide the techniques to be reviewed into two categories, *extensional* and *intensional.* By extensional, we mean techniques that describe a relationship essentially as a set of point mappings, often in a tabular format, whereas an intensional representation permits generation of members of a relation without explicitly enumerating them.

Extensional Representations

Forbus uses an extensional relationship representation, called a *correspondence*, in QP theory to supplement the qualitative influence descriptions. A *correspondence* is a point mapping for a particular set of parameters. For example, the fact that the tension in a rubber band is zero when at its *rest length* would be expressed in QP theory as a correspondence between length having the value of the rest length and tension having the value zero.

```
(Correspondence  (A (tension band))  Zero
                 (A (length band))   (A (rest-length band)))
```

Since QP theory does not make direct use of actual parameter magnitudes, the primary import of a correspondence is to permit ordering information to be propagated through influences. For example, given the above correspondence together with the fact that the tension is qualitatively proportional to the length, we can deduce that, if the length of the rubber band is greater than its rest length, its tension must be greater than zero.

Agogino [AR86] has developed a process-monitoring and diagnosis framework based on influence diagrams [Mil76], the Influence Diagram Expert System (IDES). In this system, influence arcs similar to those presented in the influence dependency graphs in Chapter 4 are annotated with probabilistic mappings of discretized value spaces for the variables participating in the arcs. The use of conditional probabilities in this way is well understood, and as a result the graphs and mappings can be transformed dynamically, depending on the knowns and unknowns in a particular query. The graph is called the *relational* level of description, and the conditional probabilities are referred to as the *numerical* level of description of the relationship. Introduced is the notion that relationships can be characterized at various levels, with different inferences possible, given each level of characterization. However, this idea has not yet actually been explored in IDES

- all action takes place at the numerical level. Although this approach offers interesting possibilities for smoothly extending QP theory functional representations, it has the serious disadvantage of requiring the collection of a large number of precise point probabilities to characterize each relation.

Zadeh presented a new approach to the representation and analysis of complex processes in [Zad73]. This approach, based on fuzzy representations for both parameter values and the relationships between them, has spawned a major research area in fuzzy logic control. We have reviewed this work in detail in Chapter 2. There are presented two primary representational techniques that are relevant to this research. The first is the *fuzzy relation*, which is analogous to the probabilistic mappings used in influence diagrams, but which uses degrees of membership rather than probabilities. Methods for propagating values through fuzzy relations are discussed in Chapter 6. The second technique, called the *fuzzy relational algorithm*, is a new, rule-based representation for relationships. Although the expressiveness of a set of rules is no greater than that of the tabular form, the rule-based representation has substantial benefits in knowledge acquisition and understandability. The combination of degrees of membership with a rule-based representation permits the specification of a relation to a degree of precision closely matching available knowledge, regardless of whether the actual relationship is known precisely or only approximately.

Intensional Representations

The simplest qualitative representation of a functional relationship is the simple unconditional statement that one parameter affects the value of another, either positively or negatively. This simple representation has been found of use in modeling human understanding of social systems [Axe76] and has been labeled the *relational* level of description by Howard and Matheson [HM84]. Note that this relationship is at best a *partial* functional one. It does not state that change in one variable determines the change in the other, but merely that it contributes, in some indeterminate way, to a change in the other. Usually a closed-world assumption is implicitly made (i.e., the influences explicitly represented are the only ones operative in the situation), and then a simple form of sign arithmetic like that described below for de Kleer is used to determine the effects of changes.

De Kleer [dKB84b] has extended and formalized this notion, naming it a *confluence*. A confluence is a qualitative differential equation. For example,

$$[0 < A < A_{max}] : dP + dA - dQ = 0$$

displays the relationship between the qualitative variables for pressure, area, and flow in de Kleer's model of a pressure regulator. Note that this is a full functional representation of the relationship. If we know values for two of the parameters, then the value of the third can be determined from the above expression according to the rules for qualitative addition and subtraction. These rules are shown in Fig. 5.1.

Y \ X	-	0	+
-	-	-	?
0	-	0	+
+	?	+	+

X+Y

Y \ X	-	0	+
-	+	0	-
0	0	0	0
+	-	0	+

X * Y

FIGURE 5.1. Arithmetic for Qualitative Sign Abstractions

The other major extension made by de Kleer is the addition of a conditional prefix to the confluence. The prefix "$[0 < A < A_{max}]$:" states that the confluence is only valid when A is between the stated limits. This permits modeling of nonmonotonic relationships by dividing them into a series of piecewise monotonic components.

Forbus retains the conditional component of confluences in the qualitative proportionalities and influences of QP theory, but returns to a partial functional form for relationships. This is necessitated, as discussed in Chapter 2, by his switch from a component-based to a process-based model of physical systems in change. The conditional component is removed from the individual relation and specified as the condition under which an entire set of relations holds (the quantity-conditions for an individual view or process), and each individual relation is a simple statement of partial functional dependence, as in Axelrod[Axe76].

We use fuzzy relational algorithms to supplement QP theory's functional characterizations in a way similar to that in which probabilistic mappings supplement the graphical descriptions in influence diagrams. Our approach is similar in this respect to Kosko's [Kos86]. Kosko has shown in his work on fuzzy cognitive maps the utility of fuzzy strength annotations on the arcs in the cognitive maps of Axelrod. Fuzzy relational algorithms eliminate the necessity of providing exhaustive point probabilities and permit characterization of relationships in very natural terms.

5.3 Related Work

Several research projects have investigated ways of improving simple single-level qualitative reasoning systems to reduce ambiguity.

Pan [Pan83] uses both qualitative and quantitative descriptions of parameter values in a system that reasons about dependent faults and performs ***predictive analysis***. In Forbus' terms, predictive analysis is a process of measurement interpretation, followed by limit analysis combined with matching predicted states against observed parameter values and pruning mismatched states. Although it is not completely clear from Pan's thesis, it seems that he does not use a quantity lattice but rather represents quantities either qualitatively using a simple three-value scale (−0+), or numerically using real numbers. Inference is performed using numbers if numeric values are available for all inputs; otherwise a qualitative inference is performed. The problem of matching precise numeric predictions with actual observations is handled by performing hard-coded ***approximate matches***. Time is handled quantitatively, with two classes of discrete event transitions representable, instantaneous and delayed. Delayed transitions are associated with a specific numeric time delay.

Simmons [Sim83] uses a mixed qualitative/quantitative representation for quantities in a system for reasoning about geological changes. His system uses a quantity lattice like Forbus', but extended in two ways. First, numeric values other than 0 may appear in the lattice (e.g., $X > 3.5$). Second, each variable has associated with it a numeric interval that represents the transitive closure of all ordering relations in which it participates. This permits rapid determination of some ordering relations (i.e., those where the respective intervals do not overlap) without having to search the entire network. However, maintaining the consistency and correctness of these intervals in the presence of a dynamically changing lattice is apparently problematical and time consuming. Also, dependencies need to be maintained for each inference drawn on the basis of the interval values, so that these inferences can be recomputed when the interval is updated. Finally, whereas Forbus uses a mixed propositional/lattice representation for quantities (the value of the sign is represented propositionally), Simmons used a purely lattice representation.

Rajogopalan [Raj84] applies qualitative modeling to turbojet engines. Like Pan, he supplements qualitative with quantitative information if it is available, to reduce ambiguity, and like Pan, he represents quantitative information as real numbers.

An alternate model for reasoning with semiquantitative information within a qualitative framework is described in [MS87]. In this work, the authors assume that an influence annotation represents an absolute, rather than a normalized, sensitivity. Although either method can be used to resolve influence conflicts, the method presented in this book permits semiquantitative estimates of the effects of control actions as well.

5.4 Linguistic Extensions to QP Descriptions

We have identified three types of extensions that can be made to QP theory to address the kinds of ambiguity described earlier. First, ordering relations can be extended to permit representation of uncertainty about value orderings. Second, extensions can be made to the description of functional dependencies (influences and qualitative proportionalities) to permit resolution of conflicting influences. Third, quantitative value extensions (and associated functional dependency extensions) can be made to resolve the problems of external ambiguity.

In QP theory, quantities represent continuous parameters of objects and exist in partially ordered quantity spaces. Processes are generally conditional on the ordering relations represented in these quantity spaces, where the ordering relations have binary truth values and the set of ordering relations between any two variables consists of mutually exclusive members. In order to allow representation of uncertain ordering information, we extend this ordering to a linguistic one, that is, one in which ordering relations are linguistic terms whose values are drawn from less than, equal to, greater than, much less than, approximately equal to, etc. We can then not only use this approximate or uncertain ordering information to identify possible states, but also to estimate their likelihoods.

In order to reduce the number of situations in which conflicting influences cannot be resolved, we propose extending QP theory functional descriptions with a linguistic strength annotation. Intuitively, this corresponds to distinguishing between first-order, second-order, etc., dependencies. Other kinds of information may be useful here, such as approximate descriptions of functional form (e.g., linear, polynomial, exponential), as well as classification of the kinds of interactions between partial functions. Further research is needed to identify other abstract function descriptions and evaluate their utility. However, we believe that the basic techniques used to incorporate strength information will be applicable for other characterizations of partial functions as well.

Finally, a complete approach to external ambiguity in QP theory requires not only an appropriate representation for quantitative variable values, but also sufficient information about functional dependencies to permit propagation of known values through those dependencies. Much work is needed to develop a suitable general scheme for this problem, but we propose here a framework for handling a subcase of wide applicability, where the dependencies for any one variable are assumed to be independent and related additively. The framework proposed is a linguistic extension to classic small-signal or perturbation analysis and assumes that changes can be modeled as differentials. We term this style of analysis *linguistic perturbation* (LP) analysis.

In order to represent the quantitative aspect of a quantity value, the value space for a variable is extended from $\{-, 0, +\}$ to a full discretized basis set over the domain of interest. This discretized basis set is treated as the internal representation of a linguistic variable describing the quantity's amount. Two critical issues raised by this approach are the integration of this representation with the partial ordering of quantities, and the source of the discretization. The first is considered along with the quantity space extensions in Chapter 7; the second issue is treated in Chapter 9.

Functional dependencies between differentials are already represented in QP theory as qualitative proportionalities ($Q+/Q-$) and Influences ($I+/I-$), and the linguistic strength extension mentioned above will serve to reduce ambiguity in LP analysis, as well as in influence resolution. An extension of the correspondence relation can be used to establish the base conditions around which the differential analysis is performed. The complete procedure for performing linguistic perturbation analysis is presented in chapter 9.

6

Linguistic Variables

6.1 Introduction to Linguistic Variables

Linguistic variables [Zad75a], [Zad75b], [Zad75c] are variables that take linguistic terms as their values. The linguistic variable can be used as a quantitative extension of the quantity space representation for continuous parameters used in QP theory, and it can be used to reduce ambiguity stemming from all of the sources within QP theory identified earlier. Linguistic variables permit us to say that the moisture content of the shale is *low*, instead of merely saying that it is > 0, as QP theory would provide, or 21.2%, as an overprecise numerical theory might require. In addition, linguistic variables provide a natural representational mechanism for other kinds of soft, semiquantitative information, such as characterizations of partial functional relationships between parameters. In the remainder of this section we describe further the concept of a linguistic variable.

In the above example, ***moisture content*** is a linguistic variable and is assigned the term *low* as its value. The ***terms*** that can be assigned as values to linguistic variables are drawn from a ***term set***, which is generated by a syntactic rule associated with the variable. If we assume that the linguistic variable is a characterization for an underlying numeric variable, then the meaning of a term can be defined to be a fuzzy set of the ***basis set*** (a discretization of the range of the underlying numeric variable). The syntax rule for generating terms starts with a set of ***primitive*** terms whose meaning is provided by definition. The meaning of any nonprimitive term can be computed from the predefined meanings of the primitive terms by applying the ***hedges*** and ***connectives*** defined in the syntactic rule according to a semantic rule associated with the linguistic variable. A hedge [Lak72] can be defined as a function of one argument, which maps fuzzy sets of the universe of discourse of the underlying numeric variable into fuzzy sets over that same domain. Connectives can be similarly defined, except that a connective is a function of two arguments. Typical function definitions are shown in Fig 6.1 ($\vee$ is the max operator, and $\wedge$ is min).Consider the linguistic variable age. The underlying numeric variable takes values in the range [1 - 90] (years). We might choose ***young***, ***middle aged***, and ***old*** as our primitive terms, ***not***, ***very***, ***more or less*** as our hedges, and ***and***, ***or*** as our connectives. Taking {10, 20, 30, 40, 50, 60, 70, 80} as our basis set, ***young*** might be defined as $\{1/10 + .8/20 + .6/30 + .4/40 + .2/50\}$; ***middle aged*** as $\{.2/30+1/40+1/50+.2/60\}$; and ***old*** as $\{.2/40+.4/50+.6/60+.8/70+1/80\}$, where the numerator of each fraction is the degree of membership of the denominator in the fuzzy set, and "+" is the set union operator.

$$
\begin{aligned}
veryA &\rightarrow (A)^2 \\
notA &\rightarrow (\sim A) \\
AandB &\rightarrow A \wedge B \\
AorB &\rightarrow A \vee B
\end{aligned}
$$

where, assuming $A = \mu_{a1}/u_{a1} + \ldots + \mu_{an}/u_{an}$, and $B = \mu_{b1}/u_{b1} + \ldots + \mu_{bm}/u_{bm}$:

$$
\begin{aligned}
(A)^2 &= (\mu_{a1})^2/u_{a1} + \ldots + (\mu_{an})^2/u_{an} \\
(\sim A) &= (1 - \mu_{a1})/u_{a1} + \ldots + (1 - \mu_{an})/u_{an} \\
A \wedge B &= \sum_u [\mu_a(u) \wedge \mu_b(u)]/u \\
A \vee B &= \sum_u [\mu_a(u) \vee \mu_b(u)]/u
\end{aligned}
$$

and using the above definitions,

$$
\begin{aligned}
\textit{very young} &= \{1/10 + .64/20 + .36/30 + .16/40 + .04/50\} \\
\textit{not young} &= \{.2/20 + .4/30 + .6/40 \\
&\quad +.8/50 + 1/60 + 1/70 + 1/80\} \\
\textit{young and middle aged} &= \{.2/30 + .4/40 + .2/50\} \\
\textit{young or middle aged} &= \{1/10 + .8/20 + .6/30 \\
&\quad +1/40 + .6/50 + .2/60\}
\end{aligned}
$$

FIGURE 6.1. Semantic Rule for a Linguistic Variable

A simple syntactic rule for generating the complete term set can be expressed as a production system, as shown in Fig. 6.2, and can generate terms of the form ***young, middle aged, old, very young, not very young, young or middle aged, not very young and not very old***, and so on.

The meanings of these terms are defined by the meanings of the primary terms they contain, modified by the hedges and connectives as defined in the semantic rule provided with the variable.

$T \rightarrow A$	$A \rightarrow A and B$	$C \rightarrow (T)$	$D \rightarrow very D$
$T \rightarrow T or A$	$B \rightarrow C$	$C \rightarrow D$	$E \rightarrow very E$
$A \rightarrow B$	$B \rightarrow not C$	$C \rightarrow E$	$D \rightarrow young$
$E \rightarrow old$			

FIGURE 6.2. Syntactic Rule as a Production System

6.2 Approximate Reasoning and the Compositional Rule of Inference.

The compositional rule of inference [Zad75b] provides a way of computing the consequences of

$$A \rightarrow B$$

when we do not know A exactly, but some fact A^* which approximates A. For example:

John is *not young*.
If John is *old*, then his hair is *gray*.

John's hair is *more-or-less gray*.

Implication in the fuzzy case can be generalized as

$$A \rightarrow B \text{ is equivalent to: } A\mathbf{X}B + \sim A\mathbf{X}V$$

That is, $A \rightarrow B$ defines a restriction on the possibilities of values in $A\mathbf{X}B$: $(A \rightarrow B)_{ij} = A_i * B_j + \sim A_i$. Given A^*, an approximation to A, we can compute the consequence restriction in possible values for B by applying the *compositional rule of inference*:

$$A^*\mathbf{X}(A \rightarrow B), or A^*\mathbf{X}(A\mathbf{X}B + \sim A\mathbf{X}V)$$

from which we can derive that

$$\begin{aligned} B_j^* &= A^* * (A \rightarrow B)_j \\ &= \sum_i A_i^* * (A \rightarrow B)_{ij} \end{aligned}$$

$$= \sum_i A_i^* * ((A_i * B_j) + \sim A_i)$$

$$= \sum_i A_i^* * A_i * B_j + A^* * \sim A_i$$

Applying this to the above example, if we assume that hair grayness is an ordered attribute with a basis set in terms of percentage of gray hair {0 20 40 60 80 100}, and that *gray* is the fuzzy set {.4/60 + .7/80 + 1/100}, then the inference rule above generates the binary relation

AGE GRAYNESS	10	20	30	40	50	60	70	80
0	1	1	1	.8	.6	.4	.2	0
20	1	1	1	.8	.6	.4	.2	0
40	1	1	1	.8	.6	.4	.2	0
60	1	1	1	.8	.6	.4	.3	.4
80	1	1	1	.8	.6	.4	.6	.7
100	1	1	1	.8	.6	.6	.8	1

Composing this with the information that John is *not young* yields {.5/0 + .5/20 + .5/40 + .5/60 + .7/80 + 1/100} as the fuzzy set describing the percentage of grayness of John's hair. Notice that this relation says nothing about the grayness of John's hair if he is young. The problem is that, in expressing the original implication, we often implicitly assume that the contrapositive also holds. That is, if John is *not old*, then his hair is *not gray*. We can achieve this effect by computing the relation expressing this joint restriction and intersecting it (taking the term by term min) with the original relation. The relation expressing the contrapositive is

AGE GRAYNESS	10	20	30	40	50	60	70	80
0	1	1	1	.8	.6	.6	.8	1
20	1	1	1	.8	.6	.6	.8	1
40	1	1	1	.8	.6	.6	.8	1
60	.6	.6	.6	.5	.4	.6	.8	1
80	.3	.3	.3	.3	.4	.6	.8	1
100	0	0	0	.2	.4	.6	.8	1

Combining this with the above, using the arithmetic product as the min operator, yields

AGE	10	20	30	40	50	60	70	80
GRAYNESS								
0	1	1	1	.64	.36	.24	.16	0
20	1	1	1	.64	.36	.24	.16	0
40	1	1	1	.64	.36	.24	.16	0
60	.6	.6	.6	.4	.24	.36	.25	.4
80	.3	.3	.3	.24	.24	.24	.45	.7
100	0	0	0	.16	.24	.36	.64	1

Composing this new relation with ***not young*** yields

John's hair grayness: $\{.4/0 + .4/20 + .4/40 + .4/60 + .7/80 + 1/100\}$

6.3 Similarity of Linguistic Variables and Relations

The need often arises to determine the degree of similarity between two linguistic assertions. For example, if two assertions are "similar," then one may imply the other. In previous work [D'A84] I found the notion of *area of overlap* a useful measure of similarity. The intuitive notion was that two assertions on the same basis set were similar to the extent that the areas under their respective possibility distributions overlapped. However, this measure is symmetrical and does not distinguish between the two assertions when one is completely contained within the other. When similarity is asymetrical in this way, we can make inferences from the contained distribution to the containing one that are not invertible. For example, everyone who is *very young* is also *young*, but the reverse is not true. This is because *young* contains *very young*. It is this sense of similarity that we now attempt to capture. We start with a simple notion of containment of intervals and build from there.

An interval $[i, j]$ contains another interval $[k, l]$ iff $i < k$ and $j > l$. An example of interval containment is shown in Fig. 6.3. Zadeh, in [Zad75a], extended this notion to the case of fuzzy sets. A fuzzy set A contains another set B iff $\mu_A(u) > \mu_B(u)$ for all u in U, that is, if the possibility of an element being a member of A is greater than or equal to the possibility of that element being a member of B, for all elements in the domain. Informally, if A contains B, then A is necessarily true if B is true. We can extend this to the fuzzy containment case by adapting the definition of containment in the following way. We shall consider a fuzzy set A to contain another fuzzy set B to the extent that $B \rightarrow A$. That is,

$$Contains(A, B) \rightarrow (B \rightarrow A).$$

From this we can derive

1. $\sim Contains(A, B) \vee (B \rightarrow A)$

2. $\sim Contains(A, B) \vee \sim B \vee A$

3. $(\sim B \vee A) \vee \sim Contains(A, B)$

4. $(B \wedge \sim A) \rightarrow \sim Contains(A, B)$

5. $(A \vee (\sim A \wedge \sim B)) \rightarrow Contains(A, B)$

It is these final forms (4 and 5) that are useful to implement the containment test. Specifically:

$$\begin{aligned} Contains(A, B) &= \wedge_i(A_i \vee \sim A_i \wedge \sim B_i) \\ \sim Contains(A, B) &= \vee_i(B_i \wedge \sim A_i) \end{aligned}$$

Alternatively, we can develop a notion of fuzzy containment based on the notion of containment of *level sets*. A level set is a nonfuzzy set consisting of the elements of a fuzzy set whose degree on membership are above some threshold. We define the possibility that a fuzzy set A contains another fuzzy set B to be one minus the maximum level set threshold for which A does not contain B, where here we test containment by standard set inclusion tests.

$$\mu_{\mathbf{C}}(A, B) = 1 - \max(\alpha)$$

for all α such that $\mathbf{C}(\alpha Levelset(A), \alpha Levelset(B))$ where $\mathbf{C}$ is the containment relation.

As shown in Fig. 6.3, it is easy to find fuzzy set pairs for which this formulation of the containment test gives overly conservative results. An alternate form, shown below, attempts to incorporate a measure of the amount by which the enclosing set fails to contain the enclosed set:

$$\mu_{A\mathbf{C}B} = 1 - \vee_u(\mu_A(u) - \mu_B(u))$$

6.4 Support-Pair Certainty

Up to this point we have assumed that the underlying representation for the fuzzy value of a linguistic variable was a simple fuzzy set. A fuzzy set represents the possible members of a set. In many situations we have additional information that we would like to include about set membership. In particular, we may have some evidence about how likely it is that various elements are set members. In the case in which we have complete likelihood information, we can treat these likelihoods as probabilities. However, the more general and more usual case is one in which we have partial information. Support Logic Programming (SLP), developed by Baldwin [Bal85a], integrates numeric certainty with a Prolog-like programming system. In the remainder of this section we introduce the support-pair certainty representation and show how it can be used to represent the values of linguistic variables.

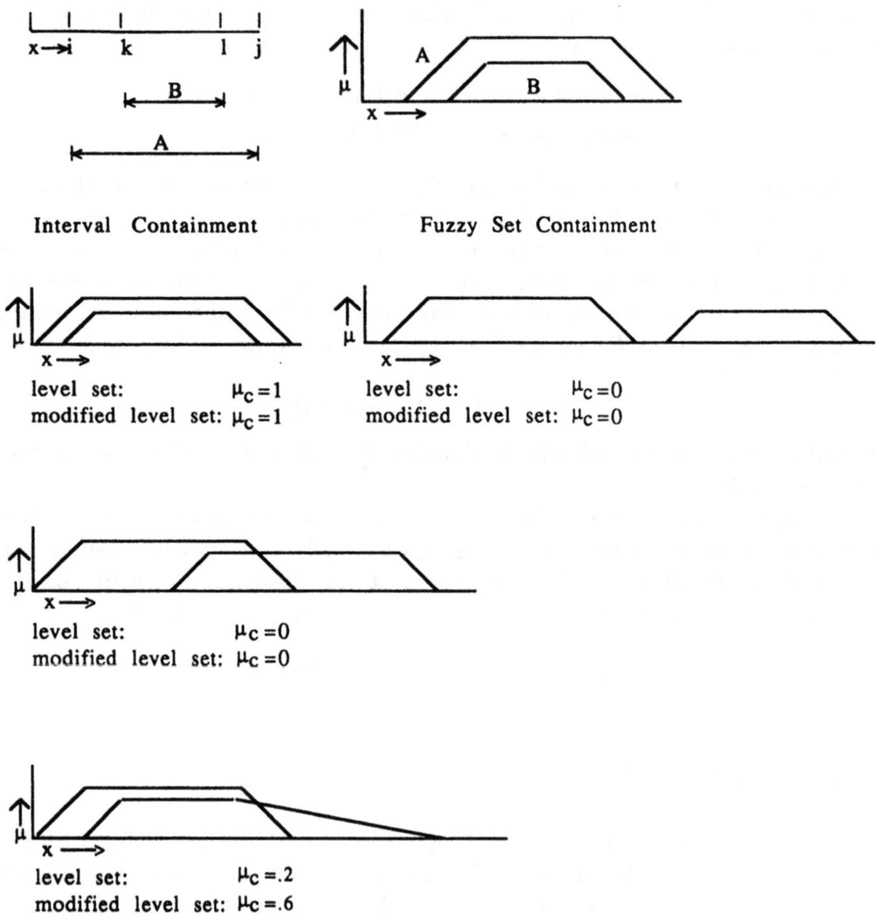

FIGURE 6.3. Containment

6.4.1 Support Logic Programming

In SLP the certainty associated with facts and rules is represented by a pair of numeric certainty values (support pair). For example

active(reaction1) : [1/4, 2/3]

is interpreted to mean that the support for the proposition active(reaction1) is 1/4, and the support for not(active(reaction1)) is 1/3. Although the support for a proposition and its negation cannot add to greater than 1, they may add to less than 1. The difference between the sum and 1 represents the degree to which we are uncertain about the likelihood of the proposition. Baldwin suggests a voting model view of support, under which we may read the above as 3 people out of 12 said the furnace was active, 4 said it was not active, and 5 were uncommitted.

There are two statement types[1]

1. $P : [Sl(P), Su(P)]$
   e.g., active(furnace) : [1/4, 2/3]
2. P :- $Q : [Sl(P \mid Q), Su(P \mid Q)]$
   e.g., direction(reactants, down) :- active(furnace) : [1, 1]

The first states that proposition P is a fact with the specified support-pair belief, and the second states an inference rule and associates a support pair describing the belief in the validity of the inference. Inference antecedents can be composite:[2]

- $Sl(X,Y) = Sl(X) * Sl(Y)$
  $Su(X,Y) = Su(X) * Su(Y)$
- $Sl(X;Y) = Sl(X) + Sl(Y) - Sl(X) * Sl(Y)$
  $Su(X;Y) = Su(X) + Su(Y) - Su(X) * Su(y)$
- $Sl(NOTX) = 1 - Su(X)$
  $Su(NOTX) = 1 - Sl(X)$

  e.g., active(furnace) : [1/4, 2/3] → (NOT active(furnace)) : [1/3, 3/4]

Inference is done as follows:

---

[1] Notation in SLP follows Prolog standards, :- is read "is implied by," X,Y should be read "X AND Y", and X;Y should be read "X OR Y"

[2] Baldwin describes two classes of algorithms in [Bal85a]. We show here the multiplication model, which was selected for its implementation simplicity. The other class of combination algorithms, based on the min-max model for *and* and *or*, does not fully specify the results of some operations and requires heuristics to select reasonable solutions.

$P:-Q$	:	$[Sl(P \mid Q), Su(P \mid Q)]$
Q	:	$[Sl(Q), Su(Q)]$
P	:	$[Sl(P \mid Q) * Sl(Q), 1-(1-Su(P \mid Q)) * Sl(Q)]$

direction(reactants, down)	:-	active(furnace) : [2/3, 1]
active(furnace)	:	[1/4, 2/3]
direction(reactants, down)	:	[1/6, 1]

Finally, supports can be combined:

P	:	[S1, U1]
P	:	[S2, U2]
P	:	[S, U]

where

$$S = (S1 * U2 + S2 * U1 - S1 * S2)/K$$
$$U = 1 - \{(1-U1)(1-S2) + (1-U2)(U1-S1)\}/K$$

and

$$K = 1 - S2 * (1-U2) - S1 * (1-U2)$$

e.g.,

active(furnace)	:	[1/4, 2/3]
active(furnace)	:	[1/2, 3/4]
active(furnace)	:	[22/37, 34/37]

Figure 6.4 shows an interpretation of this combination rule in terms of combining support in a way that minimizes uncertainty. That is, any support that one source attributes to "unknown" is assumed to be consistent with specific support assignments to true or false by the other source. Clearly inconsistent assignments of support are normalized away, and support assigned by both sources to "unknown" remains assigned to "unknown."

SLP provides a representation for truth values and algorithms for propagating those truth values through inferences to derive support for consequents. Additionally, it provides a method for combining multiple supports for a single proposition into a single composite support. It may seem that SLP represents a severe restriction of the theory of belief functions because it is restricted to representing variables with only two possible values (true and false). We shall later see how this restriction can be removed. First, we show how the compositional rule of inference for linguistic variables can be represented as a set of SLP inferences.

6.4.2 Support-Pair Certainty and Fuzzy Sets

When a fuzzy set is used to represent the value of a continuous parameter, the degree of membership associated with each element of the fuzzy set is usually taken to indicate the possibility that the element is the actual value

	P	~ P	Unknown
P	P	P and ~ P	P
~ P	P and ~ P	~ P	~ P
Unknown	P	~ P	Unknown

FIGURE 6.4. Combining Independent Bodies of Evidence

of the parameter.[3] These values are not probabilities and, in general, need not sum to 1. In fact, the sum will usually be greater than 1, since many values may be equally possible and may all have degrees of membership of 1. In some cases, however, we may have additional information we would like to represent. That is, it may be that we can further distinguish the likelihood of equally possible values. We can use the support-pair representation to further constrain the fuzzy values of linguistic variables. Taking an earlier example, rather than simply say that John's age is *not young*

$$.2/20 + .4/30 + .6/40 + .8/50 + 1/60 + 1/70 + 1/80$$

we can say

$$[0.2]/20 + [0.4]/30 + [.1.6]/40 + [.2.8]/50 + [.21]/60 + [.21]/70 + [.21]/80$$

All of the operations used earlier for fuzzy sets have been defined by Baldwin for support-pairs, with the exception of the containment test. We now consider the extension of the containment test to the case of sets represented with support-pair membership values, as in the problem illustrated in Fig. 6.5. For consistency, the result of the test should be a support pair. A straightforward way of performing this test can be developed by considering the upper and lower supports as bounding the actual fuzzy set. In

[3]This is not always the case. It may be that the parameter is varying too rapidly for measurement, and that every value in the set is the "actual" value of the parameter at one time or another

this case we can test various combinations of bounds for containment and take the most pessimistic estimate as our lower bound, or lower support for containment, and the most optimistic as our upper bound, or upper support. That is;

$$\begin{aligned} Sl(\mathrm{C}(A,B)) &= \mu_C(Sl(A), Su(B)) \\ Su(\mathrm{C}(A,B)) &= \mu_C(Su(A), Sl(B)) \end{aligned}$$

where $Sl(A)$ means the fuzzy set consisting of the elements that are members of A, taking the degree of membership of the element in $Sl(A)$ to be its lower support in A: $\mu_{Sl(A)}(u) = Sl_A(u)$, and similarly for $Su(A)$, $Sl(B)$, and $Su(B)$.

The simple fuzzy set containment test used can be any of those developed earlier. Figure 6.5 shows the results of applying these tests to a sample problem.

6.4.3 Relationship of SLP with Linguistic Variables and the Compositional Rule of Inference

If we assume a discrete representation for the linguistic variables A and B, then the compositional rule of inference described in Chapter 5,

$$(A * B + \sim A * V)$$

defines a matrix of inferences between possible values of A and possible values of B. Each of these individual inferences can be computed using the SLP inference rule described earlier. Finally, multiple sources of support for a proposition are combined using the SLP combination rule to determine a composite level of support. However, notice that the SLP combination rule assumes that the sources of support are independent. We will see in the next section that we can do better than this assumption in the context of an ATMS (assumption-based truth maintenance system, a propositional logic system used in many implmentations of QP theory).

6.5 Truth Maintenance with Numeric Certainty Estimates

The inference engine underlying most implementations of QP theory is supported by an ATMS. In this section we discuss how an ATMS can be extended to manage numeric certainty information. Certainty is represented in an ATMS by tokens called *assumptions*, which are used to represent belief

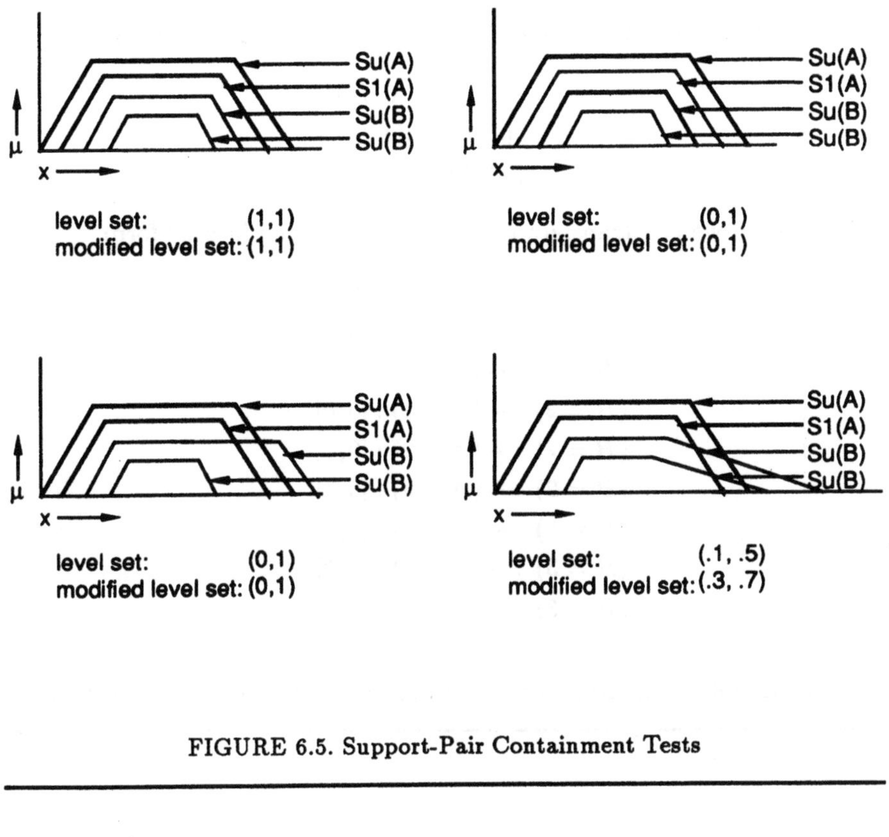

FIGURE 6.5. Support-Pair Containment Tests

If $A = \{1 , 2 , 3\}$ and $B = \{1, 2, 3\}$ and $A > B$, where

$$\begin{array}{ll} >: & \mid [0,1][0,1][0,1] \mid \\ & \mid [0,0][0,1][0,1] \mid \\ & \mid [0,0][0,0][0,1] \mid \end{array}$$

then we can translate this into the following in SLP form

$$\begin{array}{l} (B=1)\ :-(A=1):[0,1] \\ (B=1)\ :-(A=2):[0,1] \\ (B=1)\ :-(A=3):[0,1] \\ (B=2)\ :-(A=1):[0,0] \\ (B=2)\ :-(A=2):[0,1] \\ (B=2)\ :-(A=3):[0,1] \\ (B=3)\ :-(A=1):[0,0] \\ (B=3)\ :-(A=2):[0,0] \\ (B=3)\ :-(A=3):[0,1] \end{array}$$

FIGURE 6.6. Composition Rule of Inference as a Set of SLP Implications

in uncertain facts. Given a set of assumptions and a set of inferences that can be drawn from these assumptions and their consequents, the ATMS derives a complete Boolean expression (*label*) for the truth value of every proposition in the database, expressed in terms of the original assumption tokens. Heretofore, assumptions have always been taken to be truth variables ranging over Boolean truth values. This section describes a method of attaching numeric certainty estimates to assumptions and deriving numeric truth values from the labels of ATMS propositions. This technique has several major advantages over conventional methods for performing inference with numeric certainty estimates, including improved management of dependent and partially independent evidence, faster run-time evaluation of propositional certainties, and the ability to query the certainty value of a proposition from multiple perspectives.

6.5.1 Review of Methods for Uncertainty Management in AI

Standard mechanisms for performing inference with numeric certainty values, such as that used in Mycin [BS84], rely on a numeric combination of evidence at each stage of inference. This means that the source of each derived support is lost, and independence assumptions must be made in order to combine evidence from multiple inferences supporting a single proposition. Also, since the end result of inference is a single numeric value for each proposition, it is not possible to determine the sensitivity of consequent certainty values to individual pieces of evidence without redoing the entire inference process. Recently, interest has grown in attempts to represent uncertainty symbolically [Doy79], [Liu86]. In this section we present a novel method for computing the certainty of derived propositions from numeric certainty information for the initial evidence, based on the mechanisms of an ATMS [dK86a] , [dK86b], [dK86c] and the Dempster/Shafer theory of evidence [Sha76]. The method relies on the propagation mechanisms in an ATMS to perform most evidence combination operations symbolically and only substitutes numeric values when asked for the certainty of a proposition. Advantages include improved handling of nonindependent evidence, very fast run-time evaluation of propositional certainties, incremental updating of consequent certainties in response to new evidence, even after inference is complete, and the ability to request the certainty value of any proposition from several perspectives.

6.5.2 Assumption-Based Truth Maintenance

An ATMS is a form of propositional truth maintenance system [Doy79], [McA80] in which all of the assumptions supporting a proposition are explicitly recorded with it. Specifically, the label of a proposition is a list of sets of assumptions, where the proposition is held to be true if all of the assumptions in at least one of the sets are true.

A proposition gets its label via assumption set propagation through propositional instantiations of inferences called *justifications.* This propagation can be considered a two-stage process. First, each new assumption set is propagated through each justification for which the proposition it supports is an antecedent. Second, the assumption sets arriving at consequent propositions are combined with those already in the label set for the consequent. If this combination results in adding an assumption set to the label of the consequent proposition, this can then start a new round of propagation. We detail each of these steps in turn.

Propagating Assumption Sets Through Justifications

When a proposition gets a new assumption set in its label, that set is immediately passed on to each of the justifications that name the proposition as an antecedent. The justification then combines that assumption set with assumption sets from each of its other antecedents to generate outgoing assumption sets. This combination is done in all possible ways, selecting one assumption set from each of the other antecedents' labels. For example, if a justification were to have two other antecedents, each with two assumption sets in its label, then the justification would contribute four assumption sets to the label of the consequent proposition. Again, each of these four assumption sets would be the union of the initial assumption set plus one of the assumption sets from the labels of each of the two other antecedents. As a simple example of this propagation, consider the following (see Figure 6.7): If proposition A implies proposition D, assumption a_1 supports proposition A, and the conjunction of propositions B and C also implies proposition D, with assumption a_2 supporting B and a_3 and a_4 each independently supporting C, then the label for D is $[\{a_1\}\ \{a_2a_3\}\ \{a_2a_4\}]$.

Updating Consequent Proposition Labels

The next stage of processing takes place when the consequent proposition receives each new assumption set. Each assumption set generated by the supporting justification is compared with the assumption sets already in the label of the consequent proposition. If the new assumption set is identical with or is a superset of any assumption set already in the label, it is discarded. If it is a subset of any assumption set in the label, its superset assumption sets are removed from the label. Finally, if the new assumption set has not been discarded, then it is added to the label of the consequent proposition and passed on as input to all justifications that have that proposition as an antecedent, starting a new cycle of propagation. Various heuristics are necessary to ensure that assumption set propagation

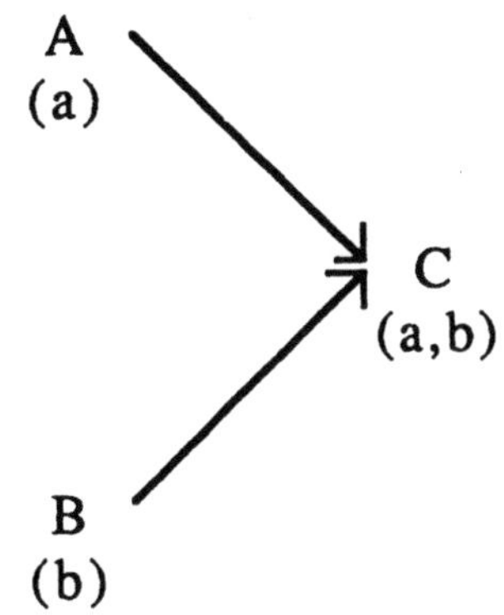

FIGURE 6.7. Simple Label Propagation in an ATMS

is efficient. The most important is to impose a ***most general first***[4] propagation order on assumption sets waiting to propagate through justifications. This ensures that effort is not wasted propagating larger assumption sets, only for them to be subsequently removed as supersets of some smaller set, and is necessary to ensure that propagation terminates in the case of cyclic justification networks.

The conclusion of a justification can be the special proposition $\perp$, and all assumption sets that get propagated to $\perp$ are marked as inconsistent. When an assumption set is marked inconsistent, it and all its supersets are removed from any labels in which they appear. Also, labels generated by conjunctive justifications are checked for consistency before propagation to consequent propositions, and they are discarded if inconsistent. This checking is performed by maintaining a database of canonical forms of assumption sets with consistency information.

This inconsistency management is used, for example, to ensure that mutually inconsistent propositions are never combined to derive support for any other proposition. Figure 6.8 shows an example of how a mutually exclusive set of propositions can be represented in an ATMS using assumptions and justifications to $\perp$.

This technique can be used to partially represent ***one-of disjunctions***. By a one-of disjunction we mean a mutually exclusive and exhaustive set of propositions, or roughly the equivalent of a Dempster/Shafer primitive

---

[4] Lowest cardinality of the assumption set.

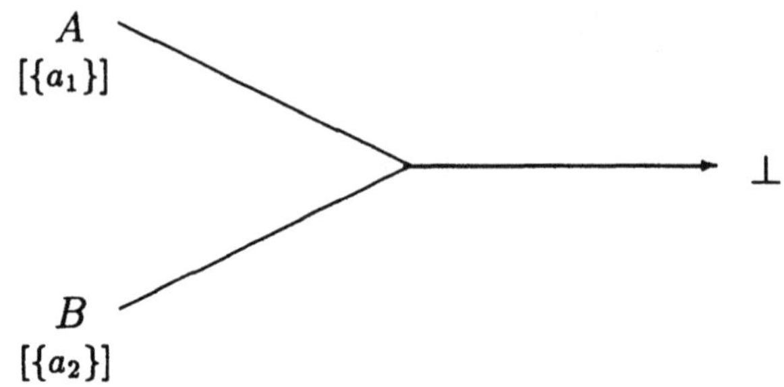

FIGURE 6.8. Representing Mutual Exclusion in an ATMS

hypothesis set. The propagation and inconsistent label management algorithms can be shown to implement a nearly complete propositional logic. Although the representation in Fig. 6.8 implies that no more than one of the propositions can be true, it does not imply that exactly one must be true. This aspect of one-of disjunctions is handled separately, by explicitly representing disjunctions in a separate data structure. The process of finding consistent assignments of truth values to assumptions is called interpretation construction. Each such assignment is called an *interpretation* and must assign true to exactly one assumption from each disjunction, consistent with all justifications installed.

Once the interpretations have been constructed, we can ask which propositions are in any interpretation. A proposition is true in an interpretation if and only if its label contains at least one assumption set that is a subset of the assumptions comprising the interpretation. We can further ask whether or not a proposition is true in a noninterpretation *environment*. An environment is simply an assumption set, and by noninterpretation we mean that it does not assign truth values to all assumptions, but only to some subset. In that case there are three possible answers. The proposition can be true in all interpretations containing the environment, in at least one such interpretation, or in no interpretations containing the environment. The first case is indicated by the proposition label having an assumption set that is a subset of the environment assumptions, the second is indicated by the proposition label having at least one assumption set that is a superset of the environment, and the third by the proposition label having no assumption set satisfying either of those tests.

One view we can take of an ATMS is as a symbolic algebra system for uncertainty information. That is, the ATMS starts with a set of uncertain data and a set of inferences that can be drawn from those data. It then computes a closed-form symbolic expression for the truth of all consequent propositions, in terms of the symbolic truth values (assumptions) of the original data. One consequence of this capability is that, once problem solving and interpretation are complete, the truth of a proposition in any solution or partial solution can readily be determined with inexpensive, purely local operations.

6.5.3 SLP and Assumption-Based Truth Maintenance

In this section we present our approach to combining symbolic and numeric approaches to truth maintenance. Although we intend eventually to incorporate the full Dempster/Shafer model in our reasoner, we have initially restricted our approach to a subset slightly larger than that incorporated in SLP.[5] Specifically, we describe below techniques for managing evidence over frames of discernment consisting only of a set of primitive hypotheses and their negations, rather than the complete power set of the primitive hypothesis set, as is treated in the full Dempster/Shafer theory. The fundamental components we must provide models for are the upper and lower supports for a proposition, the primitive hypothesis set, the frame of discernment, and the SLP rule of inference. We must then show how to derive numeric certainty values from the results of symbolic processing.

Representations for Evidence and Hypotheses

Assumptions in an ATMS represent our uncertainty about truth or falsity. We have seen that an ATMS can be viewed as a symbolic algebra system for combining certainty information. A natural extension is to integrate support-pair certainty directly with assumptions by attaching support pairs to assumptions. However, this approach is inconsistent with the basic structure of an ATMS, in which an assumption implicitly represents the belief that a proposition is true. Therefore, an assumption cannot be used to carry evidence against the proposition it supports. Evidence against a proposition must be represented as a separate assumption used to support the negation of the proposition.[6]

In the Dempster/Shafer theory of evidence, a source provides evidence

---

[5]This has since been completed but is not directly relevant to the discussion here. See [D'A88a], [D'A88b].

[6]In the special case in which the upper support is 0 or the lower support is 1, an assumption is unnecessary. If the upper support is 0, then the consequent is false, and a justification can be installed between the consequent and $\perp$. If the lower support is 1, then the consequent is unconditionally true, and a justification can be installed supporting it with an empty assumption set.

not for a single proposition, but rather distributes evidential mass over an entire frame of discernment (one such distribution is called a basic mass assignment). We can use an ATMS one-of disjunction to represent a basic mass assignment directly and to inform an ATMS that two elements from the same basic mass assignment cannot be combined conjunctively. The primitive hypothesis set can be represented by installing justifications between each pair of elements and $\perp$, as described earlier in the discussion of mutual exclusivity in an ATMS We add a data structure, a *frame*, to identify the set of propositions comprising a frame of discernment. In the case in which the primitive hypothesis set consists of only two elements, each existing proposition is the negation of the other, and therefore only two assumptions are needed to carry all the numeric information about certainties. However, in the case of a primitive hypothesis set consisting of more than two elements, explicit negation assumptions and propositions must be created. Figure 6.9 shows the complete set of assumptions and propositions for a mutually exclusive and exhaustive set of three propositions.

$$
\begin{array}{ll}
a_1 \rightarrow (A = 1) & a_{\sim 1} \rightarrow (A \sim= 1) \\
a_2 \rightarrow (A = 2) & a_{\sim 2} \rightarrow (A \sim= 2) \\
a_3 \rightarrow (A = 3) & a_{\sim 3} \rightarrow (A \sim= 3) \\
\multicolumn{2}{l}{(\text{one-of } a_1 \lor a_2 \lor a_3 \lor a_{\sim 1} \lor a_{\sim 2} \lor a_{\sim 3} \lor a_{\theta})}
\end{array}
$$

Note that a_1 is used to represent the *assumption* carrying the mass assigned to the *proposition* $(A = 1)$.

FIGURE 6.9. Assumptions for a Basic Mass Assignment

Inference

The SLP inference rule seems analogous to the ATMS justification, but again we must separate the positive and negative evidential import. As with support pairs, we can do this by splitting an inference into two justifications, one carrying the lower support of the inference and having the proposition as its consequent, and the other carrying 1.0 minus the upper support of the inference and having the negation of the proposition as its consequent. Creation of the negation justification is optional when the upper support is 1.0, and in that case the default is not to create the negation justification. Although all of this duplication may seem expensive, it has a major advantage. The original inference rule of Baldwin is not associative. As a result, each inference must combine the numeric values of its antecedent supports and provide a composite numeric support for the consequent. However, the combination rule for the simplified split justifications is associative. As a result, we can defer numeric evaluation, use the standard ATMS assumption propagation algorithm, and compute the support pair for any proposition by examining the labels of all propositions in its frame of discernment. Specifically, given

```
A:  [Sl(A), Su(B)]
B :- A : [Sl(B|A), Su(B|A)],
```

then we install justifications as shown in Fig 5.10, and derive

```
B:  [Sl(B), Su(B)],
```

where

$$\begin{aligned} Sl(B) &= Sl(A) * Sl(B \mid A) \\ Sl(\sim B) &= Sl(\sim B \mid A)) * Sl(A) \end{aligned}$$

This is exactly the same computation used in [Baldwin], and so demonstrates that this encoding correctly captures the SLP inference rule.

We now have in the label of each hypothesis a symbolic expression, in disjunctive normal form, for the evidence for that hypothesis. In the next subsections we show how these can be converted into symbolic belief functions and finally evaluated to determine the numeric value of the belief function for each hypothesis.

6.5.4 Symbolic Computation of Belief Functions

We perform one final step symbolically, the conversion of mass assignments into belief functions. This is a straightforward task; the difference is that we use the ATMS label propagation algorithms to perform this operation symbolically.

As shown in Fig. 6.11, the basic idea is to represent directly the evidential import of each primitive hypothesis and its negation on other elements in the frame of discernment. For example, evidence that A is not equal to 2 and that A is not equal to 3 is evidence that A is equal to 1. This serves two purposes. First, from the logical point of view, it ensures that every proposition in the ATMS database has a complete and correct label. It ensures that, for example, any proposition that can be inferred from the fact ($A \sim= 1$) will have in its label not just assumption sets that directly

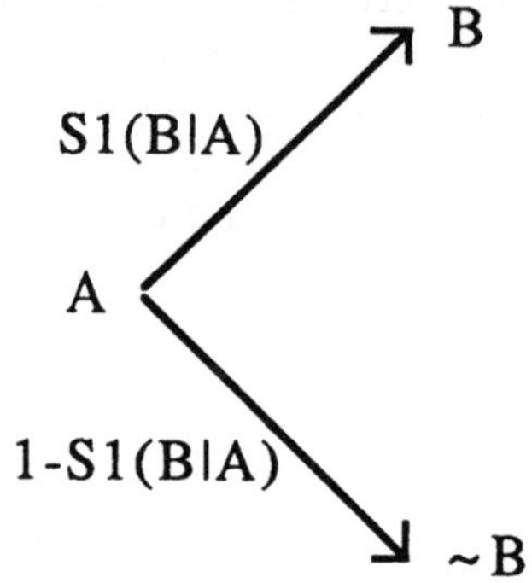

FIGURE 6.10. Representing an SLP Inference Rule in the ATMS

support ($A \sim= 1$), but also those that support ($A = 2$) or ($A = 3$). Second, from the numeric point of view, this is equivalent to computing symbolically the belief function for each hypothesis in the database.

Reduction of Labels to Numeric Belief Values

We are now ready to compute the support for any derived proposition by examining the support for the assumptions in its label. Before we proceed with the actual algorithm for performing this evaluation, three points are worth noting. First, note that most simple numeric schemes for combining uncertainty with rules are forced to make independence assumptions when combining evidence from multiple rules. We shall see that this is not true for our hybrid TMS. Because it has retained the structure of the evidence, it is able to make full use of the available dependence information when combining evidence. Second, as Heckerman and Horvitz have pointed out [HH87], simple rule schemes are unable to reason correctly about mutually exclusive hypotheses. Again, this criticism does not apply to the system presented here because of its ability to represent primitive hypothesis sets and frames of discernment directly, based on the contradiction representation ability of an ATMS. Finally, note that most simple rule-based inference systems are static one-pass systems. That is, in both the Mycin certainty propagation framework and in SLP, all evidence must be available before inference is performed. Subsequent changes in the evidence for antecedents do not affect the belief in consequents. In contrast, the propagation algorithm of the

$$(A = 1) \rightarrow (A \sim= 2)$$
$$(A = 1) \rightarrow (A \sim= 3)$$
$$(A \sim= 1) \wedge (A \sim= 2) \rightarrow (A = 3)$$
$$(A \sim= 1) \wedge (A \sim= 3) \rightarrow (A = 2)$$

$$(A = 2) \rightarrow (A \sim= 1)$$

.

.

FIGURE 6.11. Symbolic Computation of Belief Functions

ATMS is always active, and consequent labels are automatically updated in response to changes in support for antecedents. The reduction of evidence to a numeric value is viewed as a query and only performed on demand.

The algorithm we use to combine environments and derive a belief measure is as follows:

1. Compute the ***evidence space*** for the frame of discernment of interest. The evidence space is a list of every basic mass assignment an element of which appears in some environment in the label of some proposition in the frame of discernment.

2. "Complete" each environment in the label of the proposition of interest with respect to this evidence space. (e.g., if an environment is $\{a_1 b_1\}$ and the evidence space contains disjunctions a, b, and c, and c is the disjunction $\{c_1 \vee c_2 \vee c_3\}$, then the "completion" of the environment is $\{a_1 b_1 c_1 \vee a_1 b_1 c_2 \vee a_1 b_1 c_3\}$ excluding any nogoods).

3. Take the union of the completions of all environments in the label, eliminating duplicates.

4. The resulting completion of the label is a disjunction of mutually exclusive environments. Therefore, the support from the environments can simply be summed. The belief contributed from each environment can be computed using the product of the assumption masses, under the assumption that the evidence basic mass assignments are independent.

5. Compute *Kappa*, the normalization factor, by selecting that subset of the nogood database consisting of environments that includes only as-

sumptions from disjunctions in the evidence space,[7] completing them with respect to the evidence space, and computing the belief as above (except, of course, this time you do noyt discard nogoods).

6. Finally, the result can be normalized by dividing by 1-*Kappa*.

This basic algorithm is exponential in the number of sources of evidence, but linear in the size of the primitive hypothesis set when frames of discernment consist only of primitive hypotheses and their negations. Several hacks are possible to improve efficiency, such as pruning partially completed environments with zero mass and maintaining a cache of previously completed environments (since duplicates will be discarded, there is no point in computing the completion of an environment with respect to the same evidence space twice).

6.5.5 Example

Let us examine an example of use of the extended ATMS. The example is a simple assessment task in which we have a system consisting of three components and four numeric parameters. Each of the components can be in one of two states, ON or OFF. Each component state is determined by certain observable switch settings, as shown in Fig. 6.12. For example, we know that if Switch A is in the left position and Switch C is in the right position, then component X must be ON.

The problem is to determine possible overall system states given some uncertain evidence for switch settings. Figure 6.12 shows the problem description, and Fig. 6.13 shows the output generated by the hybrid reasoning system.

6.5.6 Discussion and Related Research

We have presented a technique for symbolically performing deductive inference with uncertain data, where the uncertainty is expressed numerically as distribution of a unit evidential mass over a frame of discernment consisting of a set of mutually exclusive and exhaustive hypotheses and their negations. This technique combines multiple sources of evidence in a manner consistent with Dempster/Shafer theory and uses the bookkeeping capabilities of an assumption-based truth maintenance system to improve over the evidence-handling capabilities of typical rule-based systems. In particular, dependent evidence is automatically subsumed, and partially dependent evidence is automatically expanded to identify and eliminate duplicated components. Although it is beyond the scope of this book, we note in pass-

[7] Nogoods generated by mutual exclusivity of the elements of a single basic mass assignment are *not* included!

```
;; component state frames

(mutually-exclusive '((X on) (X off)))
(mutually-exclusive '((Y on) (Y off)))
(mutually-exclusive '((Z on) (Z off)))

;; observable state frames

(mutually-exclusive
      '((Switch A left) (Switch A center) (Switch A right)))
(mutually-exclusive
      '((Switch B left) (Switch B center) (Switch B right)))
(mutually-exclusive
      '((Switch C left) (Switch C Center) (Switch C right)))

;; relations between observables and component states

(<-> ((Switch A left) (Switch C left)) ((X on)))
(<-> ((Switch A left) (Switch C center)) ((Y on)))
(<-> ((Switch A center) (Switch B center)) ((Z on)))

;; evidence - each pair is mass assigned to proposition
     and its negation.

(basic-mass-assignment '(((Switch A left) 0.27 0.0)
                         ((Switch A center) 0.61 0.0)
                         ((Switch A right) 0.0 0.12)))

(basic-mass-assignment '(((Switch B left) 0.13 0.0)
                         ((Switch B center) 0.76 0.0)
                         ((Switch B right) 0.0 0.11)))

(basic-mass-assignment '(((Switch C left) 0.87 0.0)
                         ((Switch C Center) 0.02 0.0)
                         ((Switch C right) 0.0 0.11)))
```

FIGURE 6.12. Example Problem Setup

```
Solution: (Z OFF) (Y OFF) (X ON):   [.23 , .45]
Solution: (Z OFF) (Y ON) (X OFF):   [.01 , .22]
Solution: (Z ON) (Y OFF) (X OFF):   [.46 , .68]
Solution: (Z OFF) (Y OFF) (X OFF):  [.08 , .29]
```

FIGURE 6.13. ATMS Example Results

ing that this technique can be used to represent evidential relationships between inference rules as well.

The work presented here can be seen as nothing more than a good implementation of an existing numeric technique. Although this view is not incorrect, we believe it does not go far enough. The power of the approach described here arises from the use of *multiple representations* for uncertainty. Tasks that require reasoning with uncertain information typically have two fundamental subtasks at their core.[8] The first is identification and exploration of alternative hypotheses (e.g., given that the temperature is rising; what might have caused it, what will its consequences be, and what alternatives for action do I have?). Existing numeric techniques do not address the problem of *generation and exploration* of hypothesis spaces. Symbolic techniques, such as those based on an ATMS, have been designed expressly for this purpose. Note that the solution hypothesis space in our example (the four possible solution states and their negations) is not explicitly listed in the problem statement. Rather, it is constructed dynamically by the symbolic component of the hybrid TMS. The second subtask is the ranking of or selection among hypotheses once they have been identified and explored. Here symbolic techniques fail: all they can say is that a hypothesis is necessary, possible, or inconsistent. Numeric techniques such as the Dempster/Shafer theory provide us with the needed mechanisms for evaluating and ranking hypotheses once identified. Thus, the hybrid reasoning scheme we have presented offers a more complete view of reasoning under uncertainty than any system based solely on either symbolic or numeric techniques.

[8]The following is an oversimplified model. The two subtasks are not necessarily sequential, nor do they necessarily occur only once. Nonetheless, the argument made applies to any more sophisticated model in which these two subtasks can be identified as components.

Others have begun to explore the possibility of combining symbolic and numeric approaches to uncertainty. Hanks [Han87] describes a system based on justification-based truth maintenance (JTMS) techniques which can accept numeric estimates of default likelihood, and estimate hypothesis certainties. However, since a JTMS only stores a single bit representing truth or falsity at each proposition, it seems to suffer the same limitations as typical rule-based systems such as Mycin. More interesting, we believe, is the ATMS-based approach outlined by deKleer and Williams [dKW87]. Whereas we have described a system for deductive inference, they are primarily concerned with abductive inference. Also, they assume measurements are made without uncertainty. Finally, since their scheme is based on probabilities, they cannot accept evidence for other than primitive hypotheses. In particular, they cannot accept evidence against a hypothesis. However, abductive inference within this framework is clearly an important problem. Although it is beyond the scope of this discussion, techniques presented here extend straightforwardly to abductive inference [D'A88a], [D'A88b]. See also recent work by Laskey [LL88].

6.6 Summary

This chapter has presented the basic concepts behind linguistic variables and developed some of the basic mechanisms we shall need to use linguistic representations as extensions of the quantity and function representations in QP theory. This has required developing a measure of the similarity of two linguistic variables based on a notion of containment, and developing techniques for representing linguistic variables within the propositional truth maintenance system that underlies the current implementation of QP theory.

We have presented a method for computing numeric certainty values of derived propositions from the certainty values of the assumptions on which inference was based. This method relies on the basic label propagation algorithm of an ATMS to compute closed-form symbolic certainty expressions for each proposition. The inferential structure built in the ATMS is adapted from that in support logic programming. Numeric certainty values are then computed by substituting assumption certainties into the symbolic certainty expression for the proposition of interest and evaluating the resulting expression. Advantages of this technique include improved handling of dependent and partially independent evidence, rapid reevaluation of propositional certainty values with different sets of assumption certainties, and the ability to obtain certainty values for a variety of different perspectives (partial solutions) with little computational effort.

7

Linguistic Quantity Spaces

This chapter discusses the linguistic quantity space. A linguistic quantity space is a partially ordered set of linguistic variables. The basic motivation of the linguistic quantity space is to provide a qualitative extension to the parameter value representation in QP theory. This will enable the incorporation of quantitative value measurements into measurement interpretation, as well as the estimation of the effects of continuous control actions (the latter when combined with the extended functional characterization described in the next chapter). We first describe the notion functionally, in terms of the operations it supports, and then discuss some implementation considerations. The chapter concludes with a discussion of measurement interpretation, and shows how it can be extended to include linguistic estimates of parameter magnitudes.

7.1 A Functional Overview

A linguistic quantity space provides a representation for both ordering and magnitude information about quantities. Two classes of operations can be performed in a linguistic quantity space, asserting of new information and querying the consequences of previously provided information. The assertions are either ordering relations between linguistic variables or fuzzy values for linguistic variables, and the queries are either regarding the consistency of a hypothetical ordering relation with those previously asserted, or regarding the current "best estimate" of the value of a linguistic variable. Sample legal assertions might include

(Temp flame) *much greater than* (Temp kettle)

(Temp kettle) *approximately equal to* boiling[1]

Similarly, sample queries might be

(Temp flame) *greater than* boiling ?

(Temp kettle) *less than* (Temp flame) ?

(Value (Temp kettle)) ?

---

[1] *Boiling* is a fuzzy value, not a linguistic variable.

where the first two queries return linguistic truth values, and the final query returns a linguistic temperature.

The primary terms we use in fuzzy ordering assertions and queries are *lessthan*, *equalto*, and *greaterthan*. The hedges are *approximately*, *slightly*, and *much*, and can be optionally intensified by *very*.

7.2 Computing the Consequences of a Linguistic Quantity Space

In order to describe the computation of consequences of the information in a linguistic quantity space, we must specify both the representations used and the algorithms that operate over those representations. The representations needed are those for parameter values and for ordering relations between them. There are two basic operations we need to perform:

1. Given a quantity space, deduce the implied restrictions on unknown variable values.

2. Test consistency of a proposed relation with the quantity space.

We shall treat each of these in turn and close this section with a discussion of the actual procedures that operate in our implementation of linguistic quantity spaces.

7.2.1 Representation of Parameter Values and Relations

The value of a linguistic variable is a linguistic term chosen from a term set generated by a syntactic rule, as described earlier. Internally, we represent the value of a variable as a fuzzy set of elements of the basis set. The basis set is a discretization of the domain for the underlying numeric variable. As described in the chapter on linguistic variables, the linguistic form of the value for a linguistic variable can be converted into this internal representation, given a definition of the internal representation for the primitive terms in the term set and a semantic rule for the variable.

We can use the same basic approach to represent assertions about ordering relations between variables. Internally, we represent an ordering assertion as a fuzzy set over a set of base ordering relations (similar to the basis set for a variable). In the initial implementation the base relations are *lessthan*, *equalto*, and *greaterthan*. The meaning of each base relation is defined for each domain as a joint support distribution over the possible values of the variables participating in the relation. Taking *equalto* as an example, we can define it as

$$\mu_{equalto(X,Y)}(X_i, Y_j) = \sum_{i,j}[1 + (\mid x_i - y_j \mid / a)^2]^{-1}$$

where a is a scale factor.

Base relations are actually defined using the DefInferenceMatrix form, which defines the inferences allowable from a relation over a particular discretized domain. That is, given $R(X,Y)$, we can compute $Y = X * R$. The DefInferenceMatrix form allows specification of a precomputed form of $X * R$ for all possible X's. We can then evaluate the consequences on Y for any particular value of X using the compositional rule of inference. An example is shown in Fig. 7.1. The possible values in matrix locations include a support pair, indicating the support for the inference that the value pair is supported by the relation "→", which indicates a strict implication, and "⊥", which indicates that the pair is not a member of the relation.

```
(DefInferenceMatrix lessthan (10 20 30 40 50)
    (0 1)  (0 1)  (0 1)  (0 1)  (0 1)
        ⊥  (0 1)  (0 1)  (0 1)  (0 1)
        ⊥      ⊥  (0 1)  (0 1)  (0 1)
        ⊥      ⊥      ⊥  (0 1)  (0 1)
        ⊥      ⊥      ⊥      ⊥      →
```

FIGURE 7.1. Defining an Ordering Relation Inference Matrix

An extension is to consider a richer set of primitive relations. We have also considered, for example, adding ***strictlylessthan*** and ***strictlygreaterthan*** to the set of primitive relations. Figure 7.2 shows the definition of this inference matrix over the same domain, for comparison.

7.2.2 Quantity Space Deductions

The first deduction we discuss is the deduction of restrictions on possible variable values imposed by a quantity space. We begin by noting that each ordering relation asserted in the quantity space imposes a restriction on the joint possibility distribution of the two variables involved. Given knowledge of the value of one of the variables, we can obtain a ***quantity restriction*** on the possible value of the other variable, using the inference matrix and the compositional rule of inference. That is,

(DefInferenceMatrix *strictlylessthan* (10 20 30 40 50)

⊥	(0 1)	(0 1)	(0 1)	(0 1)
⊥	⊥	(0 1)	(0 1)	(0 1)
⊥	⊥	⊥	(0 1)	(0 1)
⊥	⊥	⊥	⊥	(0 1)
⊥	⊥	⊥	⊥	⊥)

FIGURE 7.2. Definition of *strictlylessthan* over {10 20 30 40 50}

$X\ hasvalue\ A$
$X\ greaterthan\ Y$
$Y \supset A * greaterthan$
or:

$\mu_Y(i) < \vee_i(greaterthan(i,j) \wedge \mu_X(j))$

But, a variable may exist in several relationships that could potentially restrict its value, and as a result of transitivity, values for indirectly related variables may restrict the possible value of a variable. Consider the quantity space shown in Fig. 7.3 as an example.

We address the problem of multiple sources of restrictions on variable values by intersecting the separate restrictions, and we address the problem of deriving restrictions from remote values by composing the intermediate relations. Specifically, the composite restriction on the value of variable Y as a result of its participation in a quantity space is

$$Y \supset \wedge_j V_j * R_{Vj,Y}$$

where j ranges over variables in the quantity space, V_j is the value of variable j, and $R_{Vj,Y}$ is the composite relation between V_j and Y.

As before; $V * R$ can be computed as follows

$$\mu_{V2}(i) = \vee_j(\mu_{V1}(j) \wedge R(i,j))$$

and $R_1 * R_2$

$$R(i,j) = \vee_k(R_1(i,k) \wedge R_2(k,j))$$

So, considering our example,

$$A = (> * > *low) \wedge (> * < *medium) \wedge \ldots$$

A is greater than *B*
B is greater than *low*
B is approximately equal to *C*
B is less than *D*
C is greater than *E*
D is *medium*
D is greater than *E*

This set of assertions generates the following space:

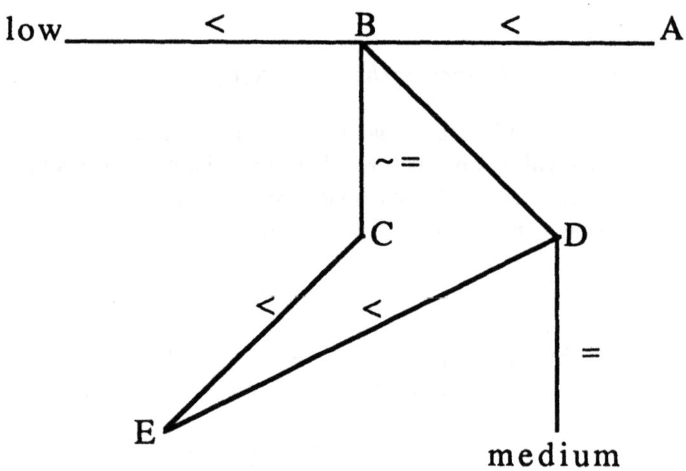

FIGURE 7.3. Sample Quantity Space

If we take a five-element basis set, 10 20 30 40 50, and define

$$\begin{aligned} low &= \{[.2,1]/10+[.2,1]/20+[.1,.6]/30+[0,.2]/40+[0,0]/50\} \\ medium &= \{[0,0]/10+[.1,.6]/20+[.4,1]/10+[.1,.6]/40 \\ &\quad +[0,0]/50\} \end{aligned}$$

then, given the above quantity space, we can derive the following restrictions on the unknown variables, where $QR(X)$ is the quantity restriction imposed on the possible value of X by the quantity space:

$$\begin{aligned} QR(A) &= \{[0,.72]/10+[0,.9]/20+[0,1]/30+[0,1]/40+[0,1]/50\} \\ QR(B) &= \{[0,.72]/10+[0,.9]/20+[.1,.8]/30+[0,.3]/40+[0,0]/50\} \\ QR(C) &= \{[0,.72]/10+[.04,.88]/20+[.06,.81]/30+[0,.7]/40+[0,1]/50\} \\ QR(E) &= \{[0,1]/10+[0,.97]/20+[0,.8]/30+[0,.3]/40+[0,0]/50]\} \end{aligned}$$

The second basic deduction is the testing of a hypothetical relationship for consistency with an existing quantity space. A consistency test can give three possible results:

1. The space might imply the query relationship (e.g., $A > B$ and $B > C$ implies $A > C$).

2. The space might be consistent with, but not imply, the query relationship (e.g., $A > B$ and $A > C$ says nothing about $B > C$).

3. The space might be inconsistent with the query relationship (e.g., $A > B$ and $B > C$ is inconsistent with $A < C$).

Note that this is completely consistent with the representational capabilities of SLP. Implication is the degree of support for the query relation, inconsistency is the degree of support for the negation, and consistency without implication is the degree to which we are unsure. Therefore, we can use the results of these tests to determine directly the upper and lower supports for the relation, subject to the restriction that whatever algorithms we use must guarantee that the support for and against the proposition never sum to greater than 1.

There are different tests for each of these results, and in addition, there are two alternate methods for performing the tests. The first approach is to compare the query relationship with the derived value restrictions obtained, using the deductions of the previous section. The second approach is to derive a ***composite relation*** between the variables named in the query relation and compare that composite relation directly with the query relation. We have already described how to derive value restrictions. We now proceed to examine how to deduce composite relations, and we shall then see how each of the three tests can be performed using each of the two approaches.

We define the composite relation imposed between two variables by a quantity space to be the min combination of the compositions of all relations on each path between the variables. That is

$$CR(X,Y) = R(X,Y) \wedge [\wedge_i R_i^*(X,Y)]$$

where CR is the composite relation between X and Y, i ranges over all the paths between X and Y in the quantity space, and R_i^* is the composition of the relations along the path:

$$R_i^*(X,Y) = R(X,Z_{i1}) * R(Z_{i1},Z_{i2}) * \dots * R(Z_{ik},Y)$$

where Z_{ij} is the jth intermediate quantity on the ith path between X and Y. We can compute the result for a two-element path composition and store it in a three-dimensional matrix, $Rc(R_1,R_2,C)$, where R_1 and R_2 are the two relations in the path, and C is the induced composite relation. Then, we can easily determine the composite of any two relations:

$$\mu_{R(X,Y)}(k) = \vee_{l,m}(\mu_{R(X,Zi)}(l) \wedge \mu_{R(Zi,Y)}(m) \wedge R_c(l,m,k))$$

R_c is the composition relation for ordering relations and is shown below for the simple ***lessthan, equalto, greaterthan*** primitive term set

	$<$	$=$	$>$
$<$	$\{1/<+0/=+0/>\}$	$\{1/<+0/=+0/>\}$	$\{1/<+1/=+1/>\}$
$=$	$\{1/<+0/=+0/>\}$	$\{0/<+1/=+0/>\}$	$\{0/<+0/=+1/>\}$
$>$	$\{1/<+1/=+1/>\}$	$\{0/<+0/=+1/>\}$	$\{0/<+0/=+1/>\}$

We can now present the two methods for performing each of the three tests (in the forms below, remember that $QR(X)$ is the quantity restriction imposed on X by the quantity space and TR is the relation we are testing):

1. Testing whether the quantity space implies a relation:
   - $Contains(QR(X)*TR, QR(Y))$ - test using quantity restrictions
   - $Contains(TR, CR)$ - test using composite relation
2. Testing whether the quantity space is consistent with a relation:
   - $Contains(QR(Y), QR(X)*TR)$ - test using quantity restrictions
   - $Contains(CR(X,Y), TR)$ - test using composite relation
3. Testing whether the quantity space is inconsistent with a relation, for both methods, is simply the negation of the consistency test.

We now illustrate the testing of relationship queries with an example, a query as to whether or not A is *greaterthan* E in the quantity space shown in Fig. 7.3. First, we show the deductions involved using the approach of testing derived-value restrictions:

1. The first step in using the method of testing derived-value restrictions is to compute a hypothetical restriction on one variable, given the known restriction on the other variable and the query relation.

   Derive a restriction on E based on the known restriction on A and the definition of *greaterthan*:

$$\begin{aligned} QR(A) &= \{[0,.72]/10 + [0,.9]/20 + [0,1]/30 \\ &\quad +[0,1]/40 + [0,1]/50\} \end{aligned}$$

$$A * greaterthan = \{[0,1]/10+[0,1]/20+[0,1]/30+[0,1]/40+[0,1]/50]\}$$

2. Test the known restriction on E compared with this derived restriction. We use the tests developed earlier in the following way:

$$\begin{aligned} Sl(A\, greaterthan\, E) &= Sl(Contains(QR(A) * greaterthan, QR(E))) \\ Su(A\, greaterthan\, E) &= Su(Contains(QR(E), QR(A) * greaterthan)) \end{aligned}$$

   Given

$$E = \{[0,1]/10 + [0,.97]/20 + [0,.8]/30 + [0,.3]/40 + [0,0]/50]\}$$

   we obtain

$$\begin{aligned} Contains(QR(A) * greaterthan, QR(E)) &: \ [0,1] \\ Contains(QR(E), QR(A) * greaterthan) &: \ [0,1] \end{aligned}$$

   and therefore

$$(A\, greaterthan\, E) : [0,1]$$

In other words, we are completely unsure of the truth of the query relation given only the evidence of the derived quantity restrictions for A and E.

The second approach to testing a query relation is to test the query against the composite relation between the variables implied by the quantity space:

1. The first step is to derive the composite relation:

$$\begin{aligned} CR(A,E) &= \wedge_i R^*(A,E) \\ CR(A,E) &= \{[0,0]/< +[0,0]/= +[1,1]/>\} \end{aligned}$$

2. Next we test the composite relation against the query relation:

$$Contains(greaterthan, CR(A, E)) : \quad [1, 1]$$
$$Contains(CR(A, E), greaterthan) : \quad [1, 1]$$

therefore

$$(A\, greaterthan\, E) : [1, 1]$$

The fact that this second procedure yielded a much stronger result shows that the derived quantity restrictions do not contain all of the information contained in the full space. Information is lost owing to the discrete representation used for parameter magnitudes. As a result, the derivation of composite relations, although computationally expensive, can be the only way to obtain unambiguous answers to some queries.

7.2.3 Implementing the Quantity Space Deductions

In this section we outline the algorithms used to perform the quantity space deductions we have described. Recall that the basic mode of inference in the ATMS is the installation of justifications (shown below as "→") between propositions. We represent the proposition that a particular variable A has as a member of its fuzzy set of possible values the discrete element a_i by the proposition

$$(A\, hasvalue\, a_i)$$

1. *Adding a new ordering relation.* When a new ordering relation $(A\, REL\, B)$ is asserted, inferences are installed between the possible values of the two variables according to the following algorithm. For each entry in the inference matrix of $(A\, REL\, B)$:
   - If entry (i, j) has value $\perp$:
     $(A\, hasvalue\, a_i) and (A\, REL\, B) \rightarrow (NOT(B\, hasvalue\, b_j))$
   - If entry (i, j) has value $\rightarrow$:
     $(A\, hasvalue\, a_i) and (A\, REL\, B) \rightarrow (B\, hasvalue\, b_j)$
   - If entry (i, j) has value $[l, u]$:
     $(A\, REL\, B) and (NOT(A\, hasvalue\, a_k))$[2] $\rightarrow (NOT(B\, hasvalue\, b_j))$
2. *Adding a new value assertion.* When a new assertion is added to the space, value propagation is performed through all the inferences described above to determine whether or not any variable values can be

[2] For all k such that entry (k,j) has value [0, 0].

further constrained as a result. Thus, quantity restrictions are always immediately available. However, composite relations are expensive to compute and so are only computed on demand.

3. *Querying a value.* Quantity restrictions are always maintained, so querying a value is simply a matter of retrieving the current quantity restriction for the variable.

4. *Querying a relation* - Quantity restrictions are always immediately available, so the quantity restriction test can be easily performed on request. However, composite relations are computed only on demand. This means that a relation query is first answered by testing the quantity restrictions. Only if the answer is ambiguous is the composite relation then computed and tested, according to the algorithms described above.

7.3 Linguistic Measurement Interpretation

Measurement interpretation [For84] is the determination of the view and process structure of a system, given a set of measurements of parameters of the system. In this section we show how linguistic information about parameter values can be incorporated into measurement interpretation. The extended measurement interpretation algorithm we use involves six steps.

1. *Elaboration.* This is the standard QP identification of all potentially applicable views and processes in a situation.

2. *Establishment of quantity spaces.* Once all potentially active views and processes have been identified, all potentially related variables are known as well. It is therefore possible to partition the variables in the situation into mutually exclusive quantity spaces. The algorithm for extracting a single quantity space from a list of all parameters in a system is shown in Fig. 7.4. This algorithm involves two procedures. The first begins with the selection of an arbitrary quantity from the list of quantities in the state. Then, all quantities directly related to the selected quantity are found by direct database query, withdrawn from the list of quantities in the state, and added to the quantity space. The next procedure is to find all of the quantities still in the list of quantities in the state that are directly related to any of the quantities added to the quantity space computed in the prevous step. These two procedures iterate until no more quantities found in the list of quantities in the state can be directly related to any quantity in the quantity space. This algorithm can be called iteratively to build a complete set of quantity spaces.

3. *Assertion of basis sets for each quantity space.* For simplicity, we use a single scale or basis set for all members of a quantity space. Once the quantity spaces have been determined, the basis set to be used for each quantity space is asserted. This triggers installation of inferences between possible values of parameters and between parameter values and ordering relations, as described earlier in this chapter.

4. *Assertion of measured quantity values.* Measurements are in terms of linguistic values. These linguistic values are converted into support pairs for each element of the basis set for the parameter measured, using the semantic rule for the parameter. We currently perform this step manually. The support pairs are then used to assign support for assumptions used to justify the elements of the basis set.

5. *Determination of view and process structure.* This step identifies sets of active processes that are consistent with the measurements. We use the standard deduction described by Forbus for this operation; the primary link between this and the linguistic measurements has already taken place in the inferences installed between pairs of possible parameter values and ordering relations in a quantity space.

6. *Estimation of view and process set support.* The standard Forbus deduction identifies sets of possibly active processes and views but does not give any indication of how likely these possible sets are. We explicitly represent each possible state of the system[3] and install in the ATMS an inference between the conjunction of process statuses implied by the state and the proposition representing the state. This permits us to obtain the likelihood of that state by requesting the support for the proposition representing the state.

An alternate form of measurement interpretation can be performed when linguistic estimates of quantity orderings are available directly. In this case step 3 above can be skipped, and step 4 is replaced by the assertion of the linguistic ordering information. An example of this process for the reaction vessel example follows. Figure 7.5 shows the code used to assert a set of uncertain orderings between heat source temperature and furnace (product) temperature, between reactant pressure in the feed bin and reactant pressure in the furnace, and between off-gas pressure in the furnace and off-gas pressure in the offtake. On the basis of this information, the linguistic measurement interpretation identifies eight possible overall process states, and determines that the most likely is state 3. A description of the full detail of each state, in terms of the status of each view or process instance in the state, is shown in Fig. 7.6.

---

[3]We mean by *state* an assignment of a value to the status of each processor view potentially active in the system.

```
(Defun extract-next-q-space (parameter-list)
  Initialize the quantity-space-parameter-list to contain
    the first parameter in the parameter list.
  Initialize the seed to the first parameter in parameter-list.
  Initialize the remaining parameter-list to
    the parameter-list minus its first element.
  Initialize the waiting-list to empty.

  (Loop
      Find all ordering relation assertions of the form
        (seed ?related-to parameter-b)

      For each such relation, if parameter-b is in the
          remaining-parameter-list,
        add it to list of parameters in the quantity space,
        add it to list of parameters waiting to serve as seed,
        remove it from remaining-parameter-list

      Remove the seed from the waiting-parameter-list

      If the waiting parameter-list is empty,
          return the quantity-space-parameter-list

        Else set seed to the first parameter in the
          waiting-parameter-list,
          and remove it from the waiting-parameter-list.))
```

FIGURE 7.4. Construction of Quantity Spaces

```
;;; We use the same DefScenario as for other examples, except
;;; that ordering assertions for the following parameters are
;;; removed and replaced with the linguistic orderings shown:

(defquantityorder '(A (Temp heater))
  '(A (Temp (c-s product furnace)))
  '((0 . 1) (.5 . .2) (.3 . .4)))
       <        =         >

(defquantityorder '(A (pressure (c-s reactants bin)))
  '(A (pressure (c-s reactants furnace)))
  '((0 . 1) (.6 . .1) (.2 . .5)))

(defquantityorder '(A (Pressure (c-s off-gas furnace)))
  '(A (pressure (c-s off-gas offtake)))
  '((0 . 1) (0.1 . 0.4) (0.8 . 0.0)))

  The system identifies 8 possible states, and computes the
following certainty values for each state on request:

(support-for '(scenario state 1)):  .01  .02
(support-for '(scenario state 2)):  .00  .08
(support-for '(scenario state 3)):  .40  .54
(support-for '(scenario state 4)):  .12  .24
(support-for '(scenario state 5)):  .00  .07
(support-for '(scenario state 6)):  .00  .07
(support-for '(scenario state 7)):  .04  .13
(support-for '(scenario state 8)):  .02  .10
```

FIGURE 7.5. Interpretation of Linguistic Quantity Ordering Information

State	View and Process Status			
1	(COUNTERCURRENT-HEAT-FLOW)	INACTIVE	.76	.92
	(REACTION)	INACTIVE	.57	.81
	(HEAT-FLOW)	INACTIVE	.57	.81
	(MATERIAL-FLOW (OFF-GAS FURNACE))	INACTIVE	.01	.13
	(MATERIAL-FLOW (REACTANTS BIN))	INACTIVE	.74	.93
2	(COUNTERCURRENT-HEAT-FLOW)	INACTIVE	.76	.92
	(REACTION)	ACTIVE	.19	.43
	(HEAT-FLOW)	ACTIVE	.19	.43
	(MATERIAL-FLOW (OFF-GAS FURNACE))	INACTIVE	.01	.13
	(MATERIAL-FLOW (REACTANTS BIN))	INACTIVE	.74	.93
3	(COUNTERCURRENT-HEAT-FLOW)	INACTIVE	.76	.92
	(REACTION)	INACTIVE	.57	.81
	(HEAT-FLOW)	INACTIVE	.57	.81
	(MATERIAL-FLOW (OFF-GAS FURNACE))	ACTIVE	.87	.91
	(MATERIAL-FLOW (REACTANTS BIN))	INACTIVE	.74	.93
4	(COUNTERCURRENT-HEAT-FLOW)	INACTIVE	.76	.92
	(REACTION)	ACTIVE	.19	.43
	(HEAT-FLOW)	ACTIVE	.19	.43
	(MATERIAL-FLOW (OFF-GAS FURNACE))	ACTIVE	.87	.99
	(MATERIAL-FLOW (REACTANTS BIN))	INACTIVE	.74	.93
5	(COUNTERCURRENT-HEAT-FLOW)	INACTIVE	.76	.92
	(REACTION)	INACTIVE	.57	.81
	(HEAT-FLOW)	INACTIVE	.57	.81
	(MATERIAL-FLOW (OFF-GAS FURNACE))	INACTIVE	.01	.13
	(MATERIAL-FLOW (REACTANTS BIN))	ACTIVE	.07	.26
6	(COUNTERCURRENT-HEAT-FLOW)	INACTIVE	.76	.92
	(REACTION)	ACTIVE	.19	.43
	(HEAT-FLOW)	ACTIVE	.19	.43
	(MATERIAL-FLOW (OFF-GAS FURNACE))	INACTIVE	.01	.13
	(MATERIAL-FLOW (REACTANTS BIN))	ACTIVE	.07	.26
7	(COUNTERCURRENT-HEAT-FLOW)	ACTIVE	.08	.24
	(REACTION)	INACTIVE	.57	.81
	(HEAT-FLOW)	INACTIVE	.57	.81
	(MATERIAL-FLOW (OFF-GAS FURNACE))	ACTIVE	.87	.99
	(MATERIAL-FLOW (REACTANTS BIN))	ACTIVE	.07	.26
8	(COUNTERCURRENT-HEAT-FLOW)	ACTIVE	.08	.24
	(REACTION)	ACTIVE	.19	.43
	(HEAT-FLOW)	ACTIVE	.19	.43
	(MATERIAL-FLOW (OFF-GAS FURNACE))	ACTIVE	.87	.99
	(MATERIAL-FLOW (REACTANTS BIN))	ACTIVE	.07	.26

FIGURE 7.6. State Details for Linguistic Measurement Interpretation

8

Characterization of Functional Relationships

We have seen that QP theory in the form proposed by Forbus is too weak to answer many of the questions we would like to ask when reasoning about a physical system for control purposes. We have proposed that this weakness be addressed by extending QP quantity and relationship representations in linguistic form using soft quantitative information. The goal of this chapter is to develop an annotation technique that will permit us to resolve ambiguities in a constructed QP model of a situation. That is, we assume that standard QP models have been applied and ambiguity has been encountered during influence resolution. What we seek here is a mechanism for annotating the models using extratheoretic information capable of resolving the ambiguity. This chapter begins with an examination of the causes of the particular ambiguities uncovered in our example. We then present a method of resolving this class of problems based on linguistic characterizations of partial functional strength and fuzzy relational algorithms. Details of the algorithms involved are presented, and we conclude with examples showing how the undecidable questions raised earlier are resolved by these techniques.

8.1 Sources of Ambiguity in QP Theory Models

We earlier identified the impoverished functional representation as a major source of ambiguity in QP theory and suggested that this could be reduced by extending the representation using strength annotations based on linguistic variables. However, the functional representations in QP theory serve multiple purposes, and it may be that the information needed to resolve ambiguity for one purpose would be inadequate for another. In order to reduce both internal and external ambiguity for both influence resolution and qualitative perturbation analysis, we must:

1. Make available the additional information needed to resolve sign conflicts.

2. Provide the characterizations needed to permit propagation of quantitative information through influences.

We address the first task using quantitative strength annotations on influences, and the second through the use of fuzzy relational algorithms as a semiquantitative extension to influences. Several comments are in order at this point. First, like Forbus, we assume that direct influences (influence statements in QP theory) are independent. However, unlike Forbus, we assume that indirect influences (derivative values propagated through Qprop statements in QP theory) are also independent. Forbus provides no explanation as to why he makes these choices, but we surmise that they are based on some intuitive sense that causes of change are more likely to be independent than change propagation paths. This seems difficult to justify mathematically. Our assumption of independence for both causes and pathways means that sign conflicts in either type of influence can be resolved given magnitude information. Second, we note that the Qprop in QP theory actually characterizes two relationships, a relationship between amounts, and another between the corresponding derivatives. Although we assume that the partial relations between derivatives are independent, we do not assume that the relationships between amounts are independent, nor do we assume that the quantitative extension of an amount relation will necessarily be identical to the extension of the corresponding derivative relation. These factors combine to make quantitative reasoning about amounts more complex than comparable reasoning about derivatives. We concentrate here on the reasoning about derivatives, which provides a foundation for later work on amounts. In the dependency chart in chapter 3 there are three basic patterns of functional relationships that prevent us from answering questions about the furnace. For each of these patterns we will seek to determine each of the following:

1. What information do we need to resolve the ambiguity encountered for each of our four goals?
2. Is that information local to a single view or process description, and if so, is it likely to be a universal feature of that view or process?
3. If information is nonlocal, or local but not universally true, how can its need be recognized, and where is it to come from?

8.1.1 Ambiguity 1 - Offgas Exit Temperature

One of the questions our QP analysis of the furnace was unable to answer was the direction of change of the off-gas temperature in the offtake, given an increase in the heat input from the heat source. The reason qualitative perturbation analysis cannot determine this change is that there are two conflicting paths through which the single input change affects the target variable (see Fig. 8.1).[1]

[1]There is a similar conflict triangle involving an indirect influence on *temp-lost*. It can be handled through techniques similar to those described here.

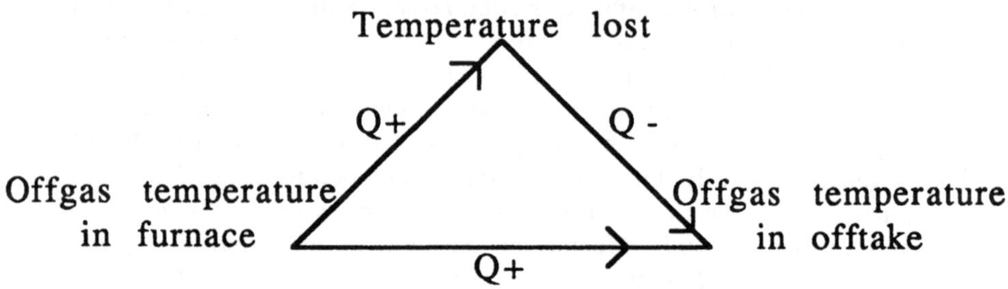

FIGURE 8.1. Ambiguity Source 1 - The Conflict Triangle

We could resolve the qualitative ambiguity if we had some way of determining that the cumulative influence reaching the off-gas temperature in the offtake via one path was greater than the influence through the other path. People performing "back-of-the-envelope" analyses of such situations will often make statements such as "the *temp-lost* is a second-order[2] effect and can be ignored here." We can model this intuition of the situation by annotating that the *strength* of the influence of the *temp-lost* on the temperature of the off-gas in the offtake is *weak*. Unannotated arcs are taken to denote a default nominal influence strength. This annotation does not capture the structural reason why this is so. We presume here that this is extra-theoretic, perhaps even simply remembered experiential knowledge about this particular system. But the annotation does provide a way of recording this knowledge, whatever its source, and using it to improve the specificity of QP analysis of the situation.

There are three influences involved in this conflict. Although more general cases of this ambiguity creating pattern of influences can involve an arbitrary number of relations in each path, three is the minimal case for this pattern, and so we refer to it as a *conflict triangle*. All of the relations in this conflict triangle come from a single instance of the countercurrent

[2]Note that it is not a formal second-order effect. Nonetheless, the frequent misuse of this formal term, even by experts, suggests that it is close to (perhaps even derived from?) a powerful intuitive notion about relationships between continuous parameters.

heat-flow view. Therefore, the annotation is local to a single model, that for countercurrent heat flow. Also, it is probably true that it is always the case that the effect of the *temp-lost* parameter is a "second-order" effect when starting from a change in temperature of the off-gas in the furnace, since the change in *temp-lost* will always be less than the original change. Therefore, for at least this case, it would seem we could add the required annotation directly to the view definition.

We need different information to propagate quantitative values through this conflict triangle. We do not need relative strengths of the different paths, but a measure of the absolute strength of each path. That is, for each link, what change can be expected in the influenced variable; given a change in the influencing variable? We need to find an approach to this problem which is intermediate between the complexities of full numerical modeling and the ambiguities of purely qualitative modeling. Again, we draw from a loose vision of "back-of-the-envelope" calculations. In approaching such a problem manually, we would first attempt to establish ranges for the parameters involved and then provide some kind of sensitivity information relative to those ranges. For example, we might say something like:

> The off-gas temperature usually varies between 90 and 200 degrees C, and the temperature in the furnace varies between 2000 and 4000 degrees C. Also, the off-gas temperature in the furnace varies proportionately to the temperature in the furnace.

The key passage above is the statement that, given the ranges defined, the off-gas temperature varies proportionately to furnace temperature. We take that to mean that, if the two ranges were normalized, then a change in the normalized furnace temperature would produce a similar change in the normalized off-gas temperature. We can model this by annotating each influence with a sensitivity value. Notice that, even though it is necessary to annotate each influence, the annotations do not require or impose global ordering information about influences. Each annotation is purely local, describing the normalized influence of one variable on the other. In the case in which the sensitivity is not constant, we can model it as a fuzzy relational algorithm rather than as a simple parameter. One problem with the approach of annotating individual influences is that it does not recognize the previous history, or source, of influences. The *weak* annotation, for example, is only valid for influences on off-gas temperature in the offtake from *temp-lost* that originate or pass through off-gas temperature in the furnace. We address this problem later in discussing the computational framework in which we embed the extended reasoning mechanisms described here.

It would be unfortunate if we needed separate annotations to solve the qualitative and quantitative ambiguities in the conflict triangle. Fortunately, the relative strength information needed to resolve the qualitative ambiguity can be derived from the sensitivity annotations by composing the sensitivities along each path. Figure 8.2 shows the annotated conflict triangle. This annotation permits correct resolution of the apparent ambiguous effect of any influence from a change in the temperature in the furnace.

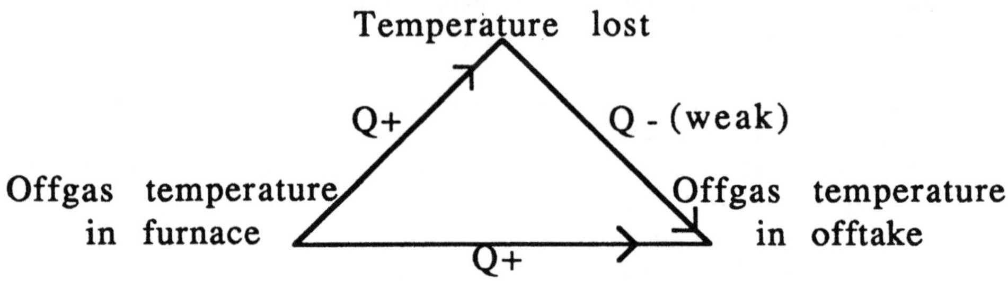

FIGURE 8.2. The Conflict Triangle Annotated with Influence Sensitivities

8.1.2 Ambiguity 2 - Product Temperature

Another ambiguity in the QP theory analysis of the furnace is in the generation rate and associated variables. This ambiguity arises not only when we ask about proposed changes, but even in the steady-state analysis of the system as shown in Fig. 8.14 at the end of this chapter. One of the causes of this ambiguity is the set of influences on product temperature shown in Fig. 8.3. Since both the *generation-rate* and the *heat-flow-rate* amounts are positive, the qualitative derivative of product temperature is undecidable. This network is similar to one Kuipers [Kui84] identifies as introducing a new *landmark value*[3] that is not in the original quantity space for the product temperature. This new value represents an equilibrium value toward which the temperature will tend. Recognition of the existence of an equilibrium value permits resolution of the effect of the conflicting influences on product temperature, depending on the assumed ordering between the actual product temperature and the equilibrium value. However, unlike Kuipers' example, in which the target parameter was bounded from

[3] A landmark value is a constant introduced into the quantity space at a point where the derivative may become zero.

both above and below, in this case there is no known lower bound for the product temperature.[4]

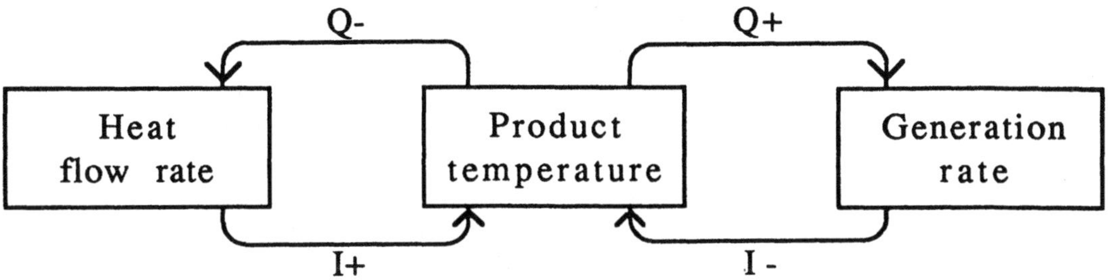

FIGURE 8.3. Ambiguity 2 - Loop Pair Case 1

Introduction of this new value enables us to determine the value of the derivative of the product temperature, depending on the assumed ordering between the current value and the equilibrium value. A heuristic that we adopt to simplify the analysis is to assume that the actual value is equal to the equilibrium value. Similar subgraphs appear around the amount of reactant and off-gas in the furnace. As a result, in our furnace example, without this heuristic the "active" state we are interested in would split into 27 possible substates.

This assumption solves the qualitative ambiguity about the derivative of the product temperature in the influence resolution of the active state of the furnace. That is, it determines that the derivative is zero. QP analysis does not encounter a similar qualitative ambiguity; it is able to determine that the product temperature will increase given an increase in heat source temperature (as shown in Fig. 8.14). It can similarly determine that the equilibrium temperature will increase. However, there are now *two* quantitative questions we might ask. The problem is that the "equilibrium value" is not a constant! It is a function of the two rates influencing the temperature. So we might ask how much it would shift, given a change in the heat source temperature. The other question we might ask is how quickly the

[4]Actually there is. If the product temperature drops below the reaction temperature of the reactants, the reaction stops and the generation-rate loops disappear. But this is not directly represented as a quantity in the influence graph. Rather, it has to be derived from the quantity conditions for the state.

product temperature will rise to the new equilibrium value.

We can roughly estimate the form of the equilibrium value change function if we know two parameters, the sensitivities of the two influence *pathways*. That is, if the *heat-flow-rate* influence is much stronger than the *generation-rate* influence on product temperature, then a change in flow rate will result in a corresponding change in temperature. Alternatively, if the *generation-rate* is the stronger influence loop, then a change in *heat-flow-rate* will have little effect on the temperature. The other question we might ask is how quickly it will rise to the new value. That is, we are interested in the derivatives of both the equilibrium value and the temperature itself.

We need two relations to characterize the situation fully. The first describes the change in equilibrium value, given changes in the two rate parameters, and has as parameters both the magnitudes of the changes and the relative strengths of the influences. The second describes the direction and rate of change of the product temperature and has the same parameters. There is also an "inertia" factor affecting the rate of change of the product temperature. In this case, the rapidity of response of the product to changes in heat-flow rates depends on the *amount* of product. Figure 8.4 shows the loop pair annotated with an equilibrium value and sensitivity annotations, including the fuzzy relational algorithm for product rate change. To maintain consistency with other annotations, we record the change in equilibrium value with the product temperature and use the derivative of the equilibrium value to store the estimate of the rate of change.

None of this information is local to any one model in the process and view vocabulary. This raises the questions of how we recognize the need for it and how it is to be provided to the system. Again, we defer this question to the section discussing the computational framework.

8.1.3 Ambiguity 3 - Material-Flow Rates

An ambiguity similar to that for product temperature occurs for the reactant and off-gas flow rates. In this case we see a similar pair of feedback loops, but the direction of the influence arrows is reversed (see Fig. 8.5). The flow-rate rate of change for the static analysis is undetermined, as is the magnitude of its response to changes in feed pressure. The ambiguity in the qualitative static analysis is due to ambiguity in the derivative of the amount of material in the furnace. This is in turn due to the fact that the amount is in the center of a type 1 loop pair, as previously noted. This ambiguity disappears when an equilibrium value for the amount is added.

Ambiguity regarding the qualitative response of the flow rate to changes in pressure requires further functional characterization to be resolved. Intuitively, if the reactant flow rate changes dramatically for small changes in input (feed bin) or output (furnace) reactant pressure, then we say that this represents an unrestricted or "free-flow" situation. In this case signifi-

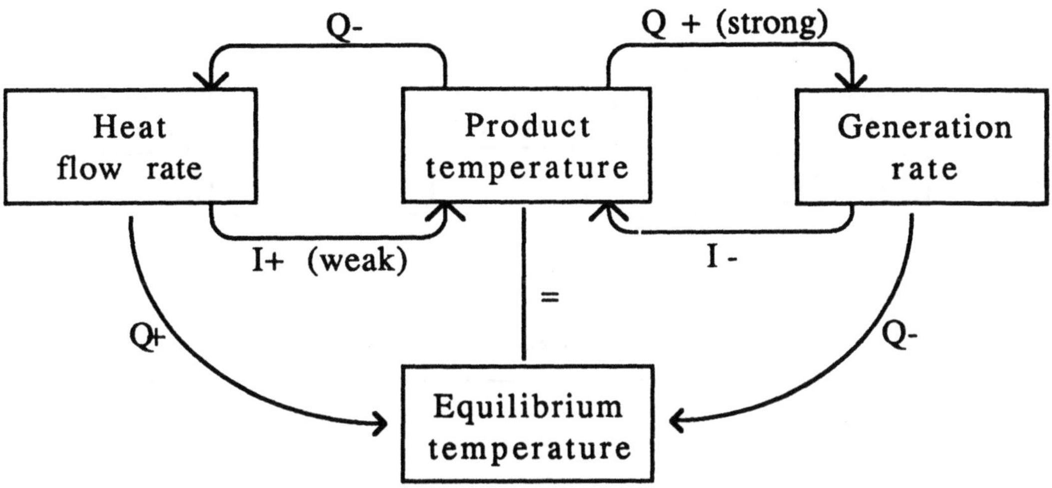


```
* Fuzzy Relational Algorithm for Flow-rate Influence on
   Equilibrium Temperature Rate of Change:

If the Flow-Rate is Zero then Iv is Zero
If the Flow-Rate is lowpos then if (Amount-of product) is small
  then Iv is pos
If Flow-Rate is pos or highpos then
  if (Amount-of product) is small or medium
  then Iv is pos
If Flow-Rate is lowpos then
  if (Amount-of product) is medium or high
  Then Iv is Zero
If Flow-Rate is highpos then if (Amount-of product) is high
  then Iv is pos
```

FIGURE 8.4. Loop Pair Type 1 - With Annotations

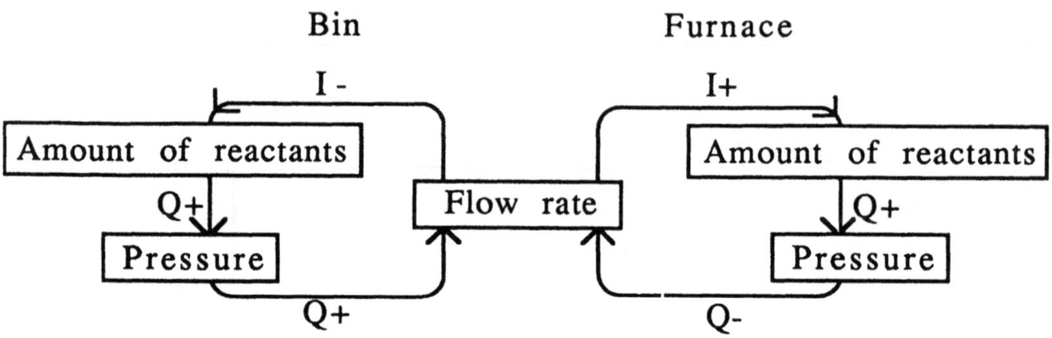

FIGURE 8.5. Ambiguity 3 - Loop Pair Type 2

cant pressure differences between the input and output can only appear as transients. Alternatively, when the flow rate is less responsive to pressure differences between input and output, we characterize this as a "restricted flow" situation, and one in which significant pressure differences can appear between input and output for extended periods of time. We can model the steady-state component of this intuition with simple sensitivity annotations on the indirect influences between the pressures and the flow rate, together with an assertion that the influences are additive. As mentioned earlier, we differ from Forbus in assuming that indirect influences are, like direct influences, additive. This is one example in which this assumption works to our advantage. The annotated type 2 loop pair is shown in Fig. 8.6.

8.1.4 Discussion

We have encountered three classes of conflict causing an influence subgraph in our example: a conflict triangle, an equilibrium-causing feedback loop (loop pair type 1), and a flow-rate-determining loop pair (loop pair type 2). We believe that each of these is a very frequently occurring pattern in models of physical systems. We suspect, in fact, that the three together account for the majority of such patterns. They are, for example, sufficient to account for the ambiguities in applying influence resolution to Forbus' models of the closed boiling situation and the fluid flow between containers. Undoubtedly, they are not complete. We do believe, however, that these

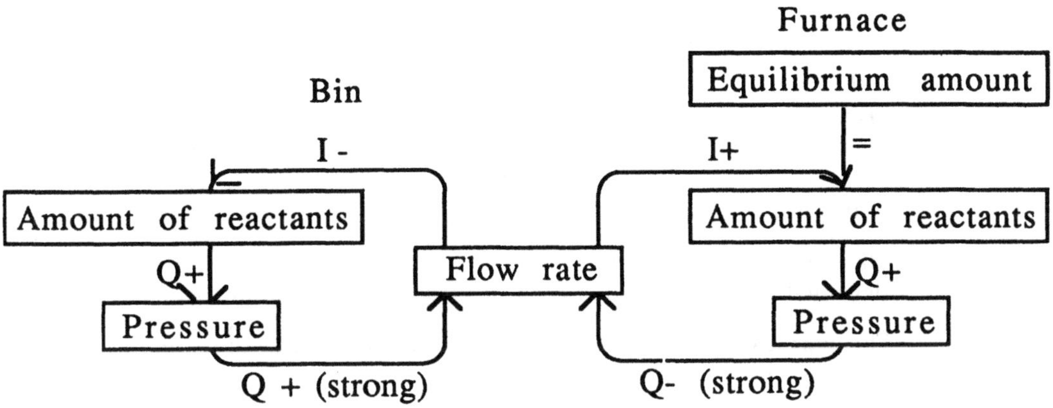

FIGURE 8.6. Loop Pair Type 2 - With Annotations

three are representative of the kinds of subgraphs that might be encountered, and that the techniques developed here are applicable to any such ambiguity-causing subgraph.

8.2 Fuzzy Relational Algorithms

Each of the three sources of ambiguity described above can be resolved when there is access to a more detailed characterization of the influences involved. Influence resolution of conflict triangles can be done, given a simple sensitivity annotation. Influence resolution for loop pair type 1 requires addition of an equilibrium value. Qualitative and linguistic perturbation analysis of these same patterns can use the same sensitivity annotation for conflict triangles. For the first feedback loop pair pattern (type 1), qualitative perturbation analysis (QPA) requires either sensitivity annotations or a multivariable fuzzy relational algorithm (in the case of an "inertia component," as mentioned earlier) to determine the change in the equilibrium value and rate of change of the target variable. Flow-rate changes (loop pair type 2) can be determined with simple sensitivity annotations. Sensitivity annotations can be modeled as parameters of a standard fuzzy relational influence algorithm, and so a single mechanism can serve to perform all the required deductions.

This section details the algorithms used to compute the consequences of these fuzzy models. In the remainder of this chapter we show how these relations are used in the context of influence resolution, to determine qualitative change values. The next chapter extends these techniques to derive both qualitative and quantitative results for an extended QPA we call *linguistic perturbation analysis.*

Remember that an influence is a qualitative partial derivative of the controlled variable with respect to the controlled variable. In QP theory, computing a value for a controlled variable takes place in two phases:

1. All of the individual influences on the controlled variable must be identified, and the effect of each of these must be computed.

2. The various effects must be combined to determine the composite effect on the controlled variable.

The above procedure relies on local propagation, rather than on global analysis, to perform influence resolution. We must extend the local propagation scheme to account for model applicability. In our extended QP theory, the applicability of particular view or process instances to a state may not be definite, owing to the ordering uncertainties allowed in linguistic quantity spaces. The above procedure for computing values of controlled variables must be modified to take this into account. The modified procedure has three phases:

1. All of the individual influences on the controlled variable must be identified, and the effect of each of these must be estimated.

2. Each of these effects must be modified according to the applicability of the view or process instance under which it was estimated.

3. The various effects must be combined to determine the composite effect on the controlled variable.

Each of these steps is described in the following discussion. If local propagation is to carry the burden of our extended influence resolution, then the propagated value must somehow be extended to represent the additional information needed. The value being propagated in influence resolution is a quantity, and the representation used is sign abstraction. Given our model of extended influences as describing the normalized sensitivity of one variable with respect to another, we can simply extend the quantity representation for the influence quantity and use a discretization similar to that used for parameter quantities to represent the normalized change of the influenced value. Although the procedure is conceptually simple, the question arises of how an appropriate discretization for this normalized change value, henceforth referred to as the influence variable, can be determined.

For the moment, assume that all influences represent linear relationships. If, then, we start with an n-level influence discretization and an m-level strength discretization, then in the worst case we might need an nm^k level discretization of the influence quantity after k propagation steps. This is clearly an unacceptable complexity. However, this worst-case complexity can be substantially reduced by three observations:

1. We are only interested in the result at a resolution equivalent to the original n-level discretization.
2. Additional detail is only relevant when two annotated influences are being combined to aid in influence resolution if they conflict. It is not the case that every influence propagation step needs to increase the number of discretization levels.
3. Failure to maintain a fully detailed discretization only increases the ambiguity of the results; it does not lead to incorrect answers. This can be ensured by specifying fuzzy relational strength algorithms that always bracket the correct answer when it is not explicitly represented. For example, if the correct result is 2.5, and the only discrete values available are 0, 1, 2, and 3, then the fuzzy relational influence algorithm should return $\{[0, 1]/2 + [0, 1]/3\}$.

8.2.1 Computing Individual Influence Effects

We begin with the algorithm for computing the effect from an influence with a sensitivity annotation. The goal is to estimate the influence on a target variable due to the value of some influencing variable, as specified by some qualitative influence relation ($Q+$, $Q-$, $I+$, or $I-$). An influence statement of the form:

$$(< influencedvar > Q+/- < influencingvar >, < influencesensitivity >)$$

is taken to specify a fuzzy relation between the three amounts:

1. C, the amount of the influencing variable,
2. S, the amount of the influence strength, and
3. Iv, the influence on the value of the influenced variable.

The value of Iv, given an influence strength S and an input variable value C, can be computed as follows:

$$Iv = \sum_{C,S} (\min(\mu_C, \mu_S, \mu_Q)/Q_{I,C,S}(C, S))$$

or

$$\mu_{Iv}(I_i) = \vee_{j,k}(\mu_C(C_j) \wedge \mu_S(S_k) \wedge \mu_Q(I_i, C_j, S_k))$$

where a default $Q_{I,C,S}$ can be generated for any discretization from:

$$Q_{I,C,S}(C_j, S_k) = sign(C_j * S_k) * (abs(C_j * S_k)^{1/2})$$

Consider the following example:

If C ranges over: [*highneg*, *lowneg*, 0, *lowpos*, *highpos*]
and S: [*strongminus*, *weakminus*, *weakplus*, *strongplus*]
and Iv: [*highneg*, *lowneg*, 0, *lowpos*, *highpos*]

and the default fuzzy relation for interpreting sensitivity annotations, $Q_{I,C,S}$, is

	$C \rightarrow$				
	highpos	*pos*	0	*neg*	*highneg*
S	*pos*	*lowpos*	0	*lowneg*	*neg*
↓	0	0	0	0	0
	neg	*lowneg*	0	*lowpos*	*pos*
	highneg	*neg*	0	*pos*	*highpos*

where

$$pos = \{[0,1]/lowpos + [0,1]/highpos\}$$

Then, given that $C = [1,1]/highpos$ and $S = [1,1]/strongplus$, we can derive that $Iv = [1,1]/highpos$.

8.2.2 Adjusting for Description Applicability

The simplest way to account for fuzzy description applicability is to treat the influence as the consequent of an inference rule, where the antecedent is the conjunction of the description applicability tests. Assuming the general form of this rule is

If Antecedent is true then consequent, or

$$A \rightarrow B \Longleftrightarrow A * B + \sim A * V$$

Then we can apply the compositional rule of inference to obtain

$$Iv_{adjusted} = \sum max(\mu_{not\,true}(A^*), min(\mu_{true}(A^*), \mu_{Iv}))/Iv$$

where A^* is the computed applicability of the enclosing description and the result must be normalized following computation.

However, using the sole mechanism assumption, that the arc used to compute the unadjusted influence is the only source of this influence and that it is otherwise zero, we can derive a stronger result:

$$A \rightarrow B \Longleftrightarrow A * B + \sim A * 0$$

For the five-level differential scale used earlier, this gives

$$\begin{aligned}
\mu_{adj}(--) &= \mu(--) \wedge \mu(Active) \\
\mu_{adj}(-) &= \mu(-) \vee ((1-\mu(Active)) \wedge \mu(--)) \\
\mu_{adj}(0) &= \mu(0) \vee (1-\mu(Active)) \\
\mu_{adj}(+) &= \mu(+) \vee ((1-\mu(Active)) \wedge \mu(++)) \\
\mu_{adj}(++) &= \mu(++) \wedge \mu(Active)
\end{aligned}$$

And, continuing our example, if the truth value of

$$(Status < Enclosing\,process\,or\,view\,instance >)$$

was [.4, .8], then:

$$\begin{aligned}
Iv &= \{[1,1]/highpos\}\&\mu(Active) = [.4,.8] \\
\rightarrow AdjustedIv &= \{[.4,.8]/highpos + [.0,.6]/lowpos + [.0,.6]/0\}
\end{aligned}$$

The results of this process are illustrated graphically in Figure 8.7.

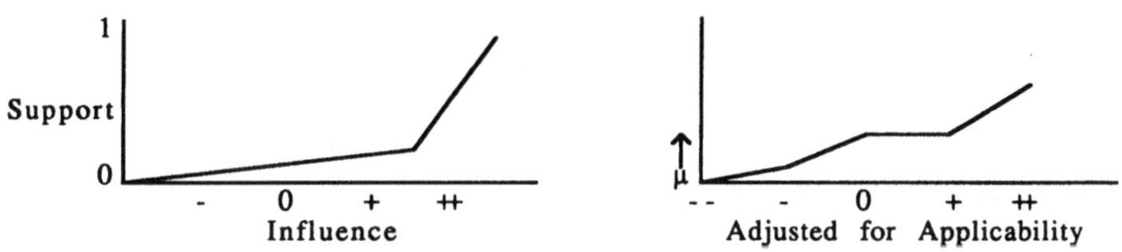

FIGURE 8.7. Adjusting for Applicability

8.2.3 Combining Influence Effects

Influences can be combined using a simple union operator, which is the fuzzy extension of the sign arithmetic used by Forbus.

$$V_{combined} = \sum_{alleffects} Iv_{adjusted}$$

This is the form of combination that must be used if we do not assume additivity of influences. Forbus does assume additivity of direct influences and uses ordering information between influence magnitudes to attempt to prove that the magnitude of the sum of the positive influences is greater than the magnitude of the sum of the negative influences, or vice versa. However, this inference is invalid because it attempts to compare the magnitudes of the influencing variables, rather than the magnitudes of their respective influences.

Sensitivity annotations provide us with a means of estimating influence magnitudes, which are directly comparable. Therefore, we can use a stronger form of influence combination that relies on influence strength to resolve conflicting effects. Figure 8.8 shows this algorithm for the seven-element influence representation used in our implementation. A rough translation is that an element is definitely a member of the set of values for the combined influence if that element is a member of the value sets for both input values; or if it is a member of the value set for one input, and a weaker element of the same sign is a member of the value set for the other input. Also, an element of the discretization may be an element of the result set under two conditions: first, if it is a member of the value set for one input, and an element of the same magnitude but opposite sign is a member of the value set for the other input; and second, if an element of the same sign but greater magnitude is a member of one value set, and an element of the opposite sign and greater magnitude is a member of the other value set.

Combining a *lowpos* with an adjusted influence effect of *highneg* would then give

$$Iv_{combined} = highneg + lowpos = highneg$$

This is shown graphically in Fig. 8.9.

8.3 Annotation Management

In examining the sources of ambiguity in the reaction vessel example, we noted that many of the annotations that could resolve the ambiguities were not universally valid. In fact, we identify four levels of validity for an annotation. These validity levels are determined primarily by opportunities provided in the implementation. An interesting area for exploration, but one that we have not pursued, would be to see how well these match with the scoping restrictions on annotation information from various categories of extratheoretic knowledge providing the annotation.

1. An annotation is ***universally*** valid when it can be incorporated directly into a view or process description and correctly describes the functioning of a particular influence in all situations in which an instance of the view or process participates. This kind of annotation is extremely rare.

$$\begin{aligned}\mu_{Iv}(i) &= (\mu_{Iv1}(i) \wedge \mu_{Iv2}(i)) \\ &\vee(\vee_{j,|j|<|i|}(\mu_{Iv1}(i) \wedge \mu_{Iv2}(j)) \\ &\vee(\mu_{Iv1}(i) \wedge \mu_{Iv2}(-i) \wedge \mathit{unknown}) \\ &\vee(\vee_{j,j>i} \vee_{k,k<-i} (\mu_{Iv1}(j) \wedge \mu_{Iv2}(k) \wedge \mathit{unknown})\end{aligned}$$

Notes -

1. Subscripts i, j, k are assumed to be 0 for zero influence, increasing positive for positive influence elements, and increasing negative for negative influence elements (e.g., -3, -2, -1, 0, 1, 2, 3 for a seven-element discrete scale, with -3 the strongest negative influence representable in that scale)
2. This is only one-half - the actual algorithm is symmetrical in the two input influences.

FIGURE 8.8. Combining Influences

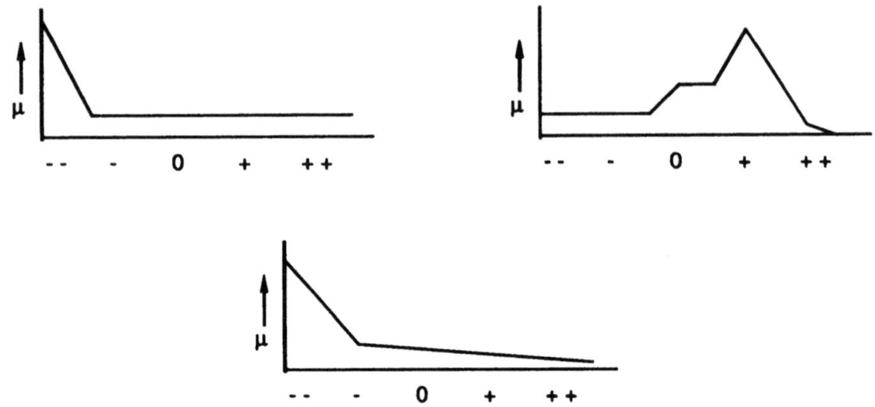

FIGURE 8.9. Combining influences graphically

2. An annotation is *scenario* valid when it correctly describes the operation of an influence in a view or process instance for all qualitative states in which the instance is active and for all valid perturbation analysis questions. These are less rare, and the flow rate and product temperature annotations are of this form.

3. An annotation is *state* valid when it correctly describes the operation of a particular influence in a view or process instance only for a defined subset of the qualitative states in which the system described in a scenario can exist.

4. An annotation is *query* valid when it correctly describes the operation of a particular influence in a view or process instance only for a particular perturbation analysis query. The conflict triangle annotation for determining off-gas temperature in the offtake is an example of this type of annotation.

The first type of annotation can simply be part of the basic view or process definition. The other three are added to the QP description of a scenario as needed during problem solving. The basic process is identical for both linguistic influence resolution and linguistic perturbation analysis, and is outlined below:

1. Execute the basic problem-solving algorithm (influence resolution or perturbation analysis). An outline of the influence resolution algorithm that we use, adapted from Forbus, is shown in Fig. 8.10.

2. Check results for ambiguities in the parameter values of interest. If all interesting parameter values are determined, problem solving is complete.

3. Otherwise, search the influence graph for known ambiguity-causing subgraphs. If one is found, and the variable for which it creates ambiguity is ambiguous (some ambiguities only show up for specific queries), annotate the graph if information on the annotation is available.

4. Once annotation is complete, reexecute the basic problem-solving algorithm.

We assume here that this algorithm is embedded in a larger system that has the necessary problem-specific information to resolve ambiguities. It also provides a problem-directed way of selecting those aspects of the larger system's problem-specific knowledge relevant to the query being processed.

8.4 Examples

In this section we present an example of the extended influence resolution for the reaction furnace. For purposes of this example, the "larger system" in which the QP reasoner is embedded is assumed to be an interactive human-machine problem solver, and so the annotation queries are directed to the human user. For ease of comparison, we include the results of the standard QP influence resolution algorithm first. Minor editing of the execution record has been done to improve readability. Figure 8.11 shows the original influence resolution output without annotations. For each quantity, it lists *amount/derivative* in qualitative terms, where "$-$: $+$" indicates undecidability. This output is the source of the first column of results in the influence resolution results (Fig. 8.14). Figure 8.12 shows the record of the annotation process. For each subgraph detected, the system identifies the critical variables and queries the user about equilibrium assumptions and influence annotations. Figure 8.13 showS the result of influence resolution with equilibrium assumptions, and finally, fig. 8.14 shows a comparison of the results with and without annotations. As can be seen in figure 8.14, annotations and equilibrium assumptions eliminate all ambiguity in the influence resolution for the main active furnace state.

```
Influence-Resolution:

  1. Determine a list of all quantities in the state
  2. Order the quantity list by dependencies
  3. Perform basic influence resolution on the quantity list
  4. If ambiguities exist, attempt annotation
       (note that this may modify the quantity list by adding
          equilibrium values)
  5. Repeat basic influence resolution

Basic Influence-Resolution:

  For each quantity in order:
    1. Perform basic influence determination as described
         earlier.
    2. If the result is ambiguous:
         select only the critical influences in the ambiguity
Attempt to prune the list using magnitude ordering facts
recombine the remaining influences
```

FIGURE 8.10. Extended Influence Resolution Algorithm

```
(TEMP (C-S REACTANTS BIN)):  + / 0
(TEMP (C-S PRODUCT FURNACE)):  + / - : +
(TEMP (C-S OFFGAS FURNACE)):  + / - : +
(AMOUNT-OF (C-S OFF-GAS OFFTAKE)): 0  /  +
(PRESSURE (C-S OFF-GAS OFFTAKE)):  + /  +
(TEMP HEATER):  + / 0
(FLOW-RATE (HEAT-FLOW)):  + / - : +
(HEAT HEATER):  + / -
(AMOUNT-OF (C-S PRODUCT FURNACE)):  + /  +
(PRESSURE (C-S PRODUCT FURNACE)):  + /  +
(AMOUNT-OF (C-S REACTANTS FURNACE)):  + / - : +
(PRESSURE (C-S REACTANTS FURNACE)):  + / - : +
(AMOUNT-OF (C-S REACTANTS BIN)):  + / -
(PRESSURE (C-S REACTANTS BIN)):  + / -
(FLOW-RATE (MATERIAL-FLOW REACTANTS)): + / - : +
(TEMP-GAINED (COUNTERCURRENT-HEAT-FLOW)):  + / - : +
(TEMP (C-S REACTANTS FURNACE)):  + / - : +
(G-RATE (REACTION)):  + / - : +
(AMOUNT-OF (C-S OFF-GAS FURNACE)):  + / - : +
(PRESSURE (C-S OFF-GAS FURNACE)):  + / - : +
(FLOW-RATE (MATERIAL-FLOW OFFGAS)): + / - : +
(TEMP-LOST (COUNTERCURRENT-HEAT-FLOW)):  + / - ; +
(TEMP (C-S OFF-GAS OFFTAKE)):  + / - : +
(REACTION-TEMP REACTANTS): 0  / 0
```

FIGURE 8.11. Influence Resolution without Annotations

```
Ambiguities detected - Attempt to annotate?(Y or N) {\it Yes}

Possible equilibrium for:  (TEMP (C-S PRODUCT FURNACE))
 Due to action of:  (FLOW-RATE (HEAT-FLOW))
                    and (G-RATE (REACTION))
Create Equilibrium value?(Y or N) {\it Yes}
Assume equilibrium?(Y or N) {\it Yes}
Annotate paths?(Y or N) {\it No}

;;; Current subgraph rules find a few spurious patterns, such
;;; as the following

Possible equilibrium for:  (HEAT (C-S PRODUCT FURNACE))
 Due to action of:  (FLOW-RATE (HEAT-FLOW))
                    and (G-RATE (REACTION))
Create Equilibrium value?(Y or N) {\it No}
Annotate paths?(Y or N) {\it No}

Possible equilibrium for: (AMOUNT-OF (C-S REACTANTS FURNACE))
 Due to action of: (FLOW-RATE (MATERIAL-FLOW REACTANTS))
                   and (G-RATE (REACTION))
Create Equilibrium value?(Y or N) {\it Yes}
Assume equilibrium?(Y or N) {\it Yes}
Annotate paths?(Y or N) {\it No}

Possible equilibrium for: (PRESSURE (C-S OFF-GAS FURNACE))
 Due to action of:  (G-RATE (REACTION))
                    and (FLOW-RATE (MATERIAL-FLOW OFF-GAS))
Create Equilibrium value?(Y or N) {\it Yes}
Assume equilibrium?(Y or N) {\it Yes}
Annotate paths?(Y or N) {\it No}
```

FIGURE 8.12. Annotating the Influences

```
Conflict triangle among:  (TEMP (C-S OFF-GAS OFFTAKE)),
          (TEMP (C-S OFF-GAS FURNACE)),
          (TEMP-LOST (COUNTERCURRENT-HEAT-FLOW))
Do you wish to annotate it?(Y or N) {\it No}

Conflict triangle among: (TEMP (C-S REACTANTS FURNACE)),
          (TEMP (C-S REACTANTS BIN)),
          (TEMP-GAINED (COUNTERCURRENT-HEAT-FLOW))
Do you wish to annotate it?(Y or N) {\it No}

 (TEMP (C-S REACTANTS BIN)):  + / 0
 (TEMP (C-S PRODUCT FURNACE)):  + / 0
 (TEMP (C-S OFF-GAS FURNACE)):  + / 0
 (AMOUNT-OF (C-S OFF-GAS OFFTAKE)): 0  /  +
 (PRESSURE (C-S OFF-GAS OFFTAKE)):  + /  +
 (TEMP HEATER):  + / 0
 (FLOW-RATE (HEAT-FLOW)):  + / 0
 (AMOUNT-OF (C-S PRODUCT FURNACE)):  + /  +
 (PRESSURE (C-S PRODUCT FURNACE)):  + /  +
 (AMOUNT-OF (C-S REACTANTS FURNACE)):  + / 0
 (PRESSURE (C-S REACTANTS FURNACE)):  + / 0
 (AMOUNT-OF (C-S REACTANTS BIN)):  + / -
 (PRESSURE (C-S REACTANTS BIN)):  + / -
 (FLOW-RATE (MATERIAL-FLOW REACTANTS)):  + / -
 (TEMP-GAINED (COUNTERCURRENT-HEAT-FLOW)):  + /  +
 (TEMP (C-S REACTANTS FURNACE)):  + /  +
 (G-RATE (REACTION)):  + /  +
 (AMOUNT-OF (C-S OFF-GAS FURNACE)):  + / 0
 (PRESSURE (C-S OFF-GAS FURNACE)):  + / 0
 (FLOW-RATE (MATERIAL-FLOW OFF-GAS)):  + / -
 (TEMP-LOST (COUNTERCURRENT-HEAT-FLOW)):  + /  +
 (TEMP (C-S OFF-GAS OFFTAKE)):  + / -
 (REACTION-TEMP REACTANTS): 0  / 0

;;; note new equilibrium values!

 (EQ-TEMP (C-S PRODUCT FURNACE)):  + / -
 (EQ-AMOUNT-OF (C-S REACTANTS FURNACE)):  + / -
 (EQ-PRESSURE (C-S OFF-GAS FURNACE)):  + /  +
```

FIGURE 8.13. Influence Resolution with Annotations

8.5 Summary

In this chapter we have identified three basic patterns of influences that lead to ambiguity in the QP analysis of the basic active furnace state. We have then shown how modification of these patterns, by adding equilibrium values and sensitivity annotations on influence arcs, could permit resolution of the ambiguities. Finally, we have described in detail the extensions needed to the basic influence resolution algorithm in QP theory to operate on these extended descriptions. We have also shown that the modified influence resolution algorithm corrects an error in Forbus' original method for combining influences. We have then presented an extended example in which introduction of equilibrium assumptions eliminates all ambiguity in the influence resolution deduction. In the next chapter we extend these techniques further, by developing a qualitative perturbation analysis technique that permits us to answer "what if" control questions; then we extend this technique to obtain quantitative, as well as qualitative, effects of hypothetical control actions.

Parameter	Standard Influence Resolution	Extended Influence Resolution
P (reactants bin)	+/−	+/−
A (reactants bin)	+/−	+/−
T (reactants bin)	+/0	+/0
P (reactants furnace)	+/?	+/0
A (reactants furnace)	+/?	+/0
T (reactants furnace)	+/?	+/+
P (product furnace)	+/+	+/+
A (product furnace)	+/+	+/+
T (product furnace)	+/?	+/0
P (off-gas furnace)	+/?	+/0
A (off-gas furnace)	+/?	+/0
T (off-gas furnace)	+/?	+/0
P (off-gas offtake)	+/+	+/+
A (off-gas offtake)	0/+	0/+
T (off-gas offtake)	+/?	+/−
Temperature (heater)	+/0	+/0
Flow-Rate (reactants)	+/?	+/−
Flow-Rate (off-gas)	+/?	+/−
Flow-Rate (heat)	+/?	+/0
G-Rate (reaction)	+/?	+/+
TemperatureLost	+/?	+/+
TemperatureGained	+/?	+/+

FIGURE 8.14. Comparison of Results of Influence Resolution

9

Qualitative Perturbation Analysis

We have seen that QP theory cannot directly answer quantitative questions about change. Yet, many approaches to process control require a means of estimating the effects of hypothetical actions. The four basic deductions of QP theory (elaboration, etc.) do not directly address this problem, even on the qualitative level. However, a relatively simple extension of influence resolution does permit qualitative analysis of the impact of control actions. The basic idea is to use the influence graph for the state of interest and perform a qualitative form of classical small-signal or perturbation analysis (QPA). The analysis is based on de Kleer's incremental qualitative (IQ) analysis [dKB84b], as is Forbus' influence resolution.

Straightforward application of this technique yields qualitative estimates of the effects of control actions subject to the same limitations as the original QP deductions. Situations can arise in which it is impossible to determine whether a target parameter value will increase or decrease following a control action. Also, many of the control actions that must be reasoned about are adjustments to continuous control parameters. Simple increase or decrease results are insufficient for reasoning about this kind of control. The same functional characterizations used to extend influence resolution in the previous chapter can also remove much of the qualitative ambiguity. An additional benefit of using these extended functional characterizations is that we can now obtain linguistic estimates of the magnitude of changes. Finally, this can be integrated with the linguistic quantity space extensions described earlier to obtain complete quantitative estimates of the effects of control actions. This last procedure we call linguistic perturbation analysis (LPA). This chapter builds up the LPA algorithm step by step, starting with the simpler qualitative perturbation analysis.

9.1 Qualitative Perturbation Analysis

Classical small-signal analysis determines a delta for a target parameter, given a delta for a control parameter. This change is determined by evaluating the partial derivative of the target with respect to the control parameter at the current value of the parameters, and multiplying that value by the control delta. A simple qualitative version of small-signal analysis would be to multiply a qualitative form of this partial derivative by the sign of the control delta. However, this is only valid as long as the change in the control parameter does not result in a change in the view and process structure for the situation. This is the qualitative equivalent of "small-signal" analysis. Therefore, a restriction on the application of this technique is that either the current view and process structure must not be dependent on any equality quantity conditions or, if it is, their validity must not be affected by the proposed change.

This procedure is simple to perform, and the partial derivatives are already represented as influences in the influence graph. De Kleer has developed a qualitative procedure for performing this computation, which he calls IQ analysis. A problem arises in determining the qualitative change values in de Kleer's confluence formalism because arcs are undirected and he allows cycles in the influence graph. This requires search to find a globally consistent solution, which he performs by introducing assumptions about unknown values and backtracking as needed.

Forbus eliminates the possibility of cycles in QP theory by fiat, claiming that cycles violate intuitive notions of causality and are unnecessary. The result of this simplification is that the search-intensive IQ algorithm of de Kleer reduces to the simple one-pass influence resolution algorithm of Forbus. An adaptation of this algorithm for qualitative perturbation analysis is shown in Fig. 9.1. This algorithm uses the derivative of each quantity to store the delta. The basic difference between this and inference resolution is that we initialize certain derivatives to nonzero values.

However, although this algorithm is adequate for influence resolution, it is inadequate for qualitative perturbation analysis. The problem is that the sign of the target parameter delta is not always the sign of the first derivative, but rather the sign of the *lowest order nonzero derivative.*[1] This fact renders the one-pass influence resolution algorithm only a partial solution to the problem of perturbation analysis. The graph of Fig. 9.2 shows the problem.

A simple analysis of this diagram according to the above algorithm would lead one to conclude that $((D(Amountproduct)) = 0)$. However, the correct answer is $((D(Amountproduct)) > 0)$. The reason is that, although the first derivative is zero, the second derivative is positive. Therefore, assuming the change persists for a finite period of time, the eventual result will be a positive first derivative and therefore a positive delta. Increasing the temperature of the reactants will increase the amount of product produced over any nonzero time interval, if all other factors are held constant. Information about second derivatives can be obtained from direct influences (I+/I−) in QP theory.

The inference sanctioned by QP theory, given that the amount of product is positively influenced directly by the generation rate, is that if the

[1] This depends critically on the state persisting for some nonzero time interval.

```
(defun Simple-QPA (delta-list)
 make a list of all quantities (amounts and first derivatives)
   in the situation, ordered by dependencies
   (this is the same as for influence resolution)

 set the value of each quantity in the delta list to the value
   specified, set all others to unknown

 For each quantity:
   If positive direct influences and no negative direct
     influences and no unknown direct influences, set
     value to positive
   If negative direct influences and no positive direct
     influences and no unknown direct influences, set
     value to negative.
   If both positive and negative direct influences, or any
     unknown direct influences, set value to unknown.
   If no direct influences, then:
     If positive indirect influences, and no negative or
       unknown indirect influences, set value to positive.
     If negative indirect influences, and no positive or
       unknown indirect influences, set value to negative.
     If both positive and negative indirect influences, set
       value to unknown.
     Else set its value to zero.
)
```

FIGURE 9.1. Simple Qualitative Perturbation Analysis Algorithm

$$Temp(reactants) - -Q+ \rightarrow G - Rate - -I+ \rightarrow Amount(product)$$
$$((D(Tempreactants)) > 0), ((D(Amountproduct))?0)$$

FIGURE 9.2. QP Sample Influence Graph

amount of the generation rate is positive, then, in the absence of conflicting influences, the *derivative* of the product amount is also positive. However, we can make the same inference for the next higher order set of values. That is, if the ***first derivative*** of the generation rate is positive, then, in the absence of conflicting influences, the ***second derivative*** of the product amount is also positive. Combining this with the qualitative perturbation analysis rule that the result of perturbation analysis is the value of the lowest nonzero derivative, we conclude that the correct result for the example of Fig. 9.2 is that the amount of product will increase, since the second derivative is the lowest order non-zero derivative. This is equivalent to treating selected direct influences ($I+/I-$) as indirect influences ($Q+/Q-$), thereby reintroducing loops into the influence graph and destroying the one-pass nature of Forbus' algorithm. A revised algorithm for QPA is shown in Fig. 9.3. The key change to the previous algorithm is that, once the previous one-pass algorithm is complete, the algorithm searches for the earliest (in terms of the quantity dependency partial order) derivative that is zero, and which has a nonzero second derivative. It then assigns that value to the first derivative, thus starting a new round of influence propagation. The procedure repeats until no such zero derivatives can be found. This is the algorithm used to derive the results shown in Fig. 4.7. Notice that this algorithm uses the same basic procedures for computing individual influences and combining them that are used in influence resolution.

9.2 Extended Perturbation Analysis

The analysis described in the previous section is capable of deriving many useful results. Our furnace example has only two independent parameters, the temperature of the heat source and the temperature of the incoming

```
defun QPA (delta-list)
 Perform Simple-QPA as described earlier.
 Execute repeatedly until no further changes occur:
   For each quantity in the quantity list:
      If quantity is a derivative and has a value of zero
         perform a higher order derivative check and set
           value according to the results.
         If value is now not zero, mark a change has occurred.
      Also, if any changes have occurred on this pass through
        quantity list, then reexecute normal influence check
        for this quantity.

defun high-order-deriv-check (quantity)

 ;;This function is only invoked on derivatives with current
 ;; value of zero.

 Set the minuslist to the list of direct negative influences
    (I- with positive derivative of influencing parameter,
     I+ with negative derivative of influencing parameter, or
     I+ or I- with unknown derivative of influencing
     parameter)
 Set the pluslist to the list of direct positive influences
 If the plus and minus lists are both empty, do nothing.
 If the pluslist is nonempty, and the minuslist is empty,
     set the quantity value to plus.
 If the minuslist is nonempty, and the pluslist is empty,
     set the quantity value to minus.
 If neither list is empty, set the quantity value to unknown.
```

FIGURE 9.3. Revised Qualitative Perturbation Analysis Algorithm

reactants.[2] Examination of the results of qualitative perturbation analysis shown in Fig. 4.7 reveals that there are some indeterminacies in the analysis, though. The sources of these ambiguities have already been discussed in the previous chapter. By replacing the basic influence computation and combination algorithm of QP theory with the extended algorithm discussed in that chapter, we can eliminate those ambiguities. Figs. 9.4 through 9.7 show the results of extended QPA using the annotations described earlier. Figure 9.2 compares these results with the results of analysis without annotations. The figures follow the same format as those for influence resolution shown in the preceding chapter, and the same comments apply, except that for brevity we omit the record of the output from analysis prior to annotation; see Fig. 9.2 for a summary. Also, only a single value is displayed for each quantity, the computed delta.

[2] Actually there is a third independent parameter, the amount of reactant in the bin. In the application that motivated this example the amount of reactant in the bin is roughly a constant, and is not considered here.

```
(EQPA '(((D (temp heater)) . ''plus'')) env)
;;; each DS2 is a record of a dx = d^2x assignment

DS2 - (D (AMOUNT-OF (C-S OFF-GAS FURNACE)))
DS2 - (D (AMOUNT-OF (C-S PRODUCT FURNACE)))
DS2 - (D (AMOUNT-OF (C-S REACTANTS FURNACE)))
DS2 - (D (AMOUNT-OF (C-S OFF-GAS OFFTAKE)))
DS2 - (D (AMOUNT-OF (C-S REACTANTS BIN)))

Ambiguities detected - Attempt to annotate?(Y or N)  YES

Conflict triangle among: (TEMP (C-S OFF-GAS OFFTAKE))
              (TEMP (C-S OFF-GAS FURNACE))
              (TEMP-LOST (COUNTERCURRENT-HEAT-FLOW))
Do you wish to annotate it?(Y or N) YES

 Can you annotate  ((TEMP (C-S OFF-GAS OFFTAKE))
                    Q+ (TEMP (C-S OFF-GAS FURNACE)))?
 (Y or N) NO

 Can you annotate
   ((TEMP (C-S OFF-GAS OFFTAKE)) Q- (TEMP-LOST ))?
 (Y or N) YES
  Globally?(Y or N) NO
  For this State only?(Y or N) NO
  For this Query only?(Y or N) YES
  Enter annotation: WEAK +

 Can you annotate
  ((TEMP-LOST ) Q+ (TEMP (C-S OFF-GAS FURNACE))) ?
(Y or N) NO

Conflict triangle among: (TEMP (C-S REACTANTS FURNACE))
              (TEMP (C-S REACTANTS BIN))
              (TEMP-GAINED (COUNTERCURRENT-HEAT-FLOW))

Do you wish to annotate it?(Y or N) NO
```

FIGURE 9.4. Annotation of EPA for Heater Temp Increase

```
;;; list uses of second derivative as they occur

DS2 - (D (AMOUNT-OF (C-S OFF-GAS FURNACE)))
DS2 - (D (AMOUNT-OF (C-S PRODUCT FURNACE)))
DS2 - (D (AMOUNT-OF (C-S REACTANTS FURNACE)))
DS2 - (D (AMOUNT-OF (C-S OFF-GAS OFFTAKE)))
DS2 - (D (AMOUNT-OF (C-S REACTANTS BIN)))

;;;  results

 (D (TEMP (C-S REACTANTS BIN))): zero
 (D (TEMP HEATER)): +
 (D (AMOUNT-OF (C-S REACTANTS BIN))): -
 (D (PRESSURE (C-S REACTANTS BIN))): -
 (D (TEMP (C-S PRODUCT FURNACE))): +
 (D (FLOW-RATE (HEAT-FLOW))): +
 (D (TEMP (C-S OFF-GAS FURNACE))): +
 (D (AMOUNT-OF (C-S PRODUCT FURNACE))): +
 (D (PRESSURE (C-S PRODUCT FURNACE))): +
 (D (AMOUNT-OF (C-S REACTANTS FURNACE))): -
 (D (PRESSURE (C-S REACTANTS FURNACE))): -
 (D (FLOW-RATE (MATERIAL-FLOW (C-S REACTANTS BIN)))): +
 (D (TEMP-GAINED (COUNTERCURRENT-HEAT-FLOW))): +
 (D (TEMP (C-S REACTANTS FURNACE))): +
 (D (G-RATE (REACTION))): +
 (D (EQ-AMOUNT-OF (C-S REACTANTS FURNACE))): -
 (D (EQ-TEMP (C-S PRODUCT FURNACE))): +
 (D (AMOUNT-OF (C-S OFF-GAS FURNACE))): +
 (D (PRESSURE (C-S OFF-GAS FURNACE))): +
 (D (AMOUNT-OF (C-S OFF-GAS OFFTAKE))): +
 (D (PRESSURE (C-S OFF-GAS OFFTAKE))): +
 (D (FLOW-RATE (MATERIAL-FLOW (C-S OFF-GAS FURNACE)))): +
 (D (EQ-PRESSURE (C-S OFF-GAS FURNACE))): zero
 (D (TEMP-LOST (COUNTERCURRENT-HEAT-FLOW))): - : +
 (D (TEMP (C-S OFF-GAS OFFTAKE))): +
 (D (REACTION-TEMP REACTANTS)): zero
```

FIGURE 9.5. Results of EPA on Heater Temp Increase

```
(EQPA '(((D (temp (c-s reactants bin))) . '+')) env)

DS2 - (D (AMOUNT-OF (C-S PRODUCT FURNACE)))
DS2 - (D (AMOUNT-OF (C-S REACTANTS FURNACE)))
DS2 - (D (AMOUNT-OF (C-S OFF-GAS FURNACE)))
DS2 - (D (AMOUNT-OF (C-S REACTANTS BIN)))
DS2 - (D (AMOUNT-OF (C-S OFF-GAS OFFTAKE)))

Ambiguities detected - Attempt to annotate?(Y or N) YES

Conflict triangle among:  (TEMP (C-S OFF-GAS OFFTAKE))
              (TEMP (C-S OFF-GAS FURNACE))
              (TEMP-LOST (COUNTERCURRENT-HEAT-FLOW))
Do you wish to annotate it?(Y or N) NO

Conflict triangle among:  (TEMP (C-S REACTANTS FURNACE))
              (TEMP (C-S REACTANTS BIN))
              (TEMP-GAINED (COUNTERCURRENT-HEAT-FLOW))
Do you wish to annotate it?(Y or N) NO

 Can you annotate  ((TEMP (C-S REACTANTS FURNACE))
                    Q+ (TEMP (C-S REACTANTS BIN))) ?
  (Y or N) NO

 Can you annotate
  ((TEMP (C-S REACTANTS FURNACE)) Q+ (TEMP-GAINED )) ?
  (Y or N) YES
  Globally?(Y or N) NO
  For this State only?(Y or N) NO
  For this Query only?(Y or N) YES
 Enter annotation: WEAK +

 Can you annotate
  ((TEMP-GAINED ) Q- (TEMP (C-S REACTANTS BIN))) ?
(Y or N) NO
```

FIGURE 9.6. Annotation for Reactant Temp Increase

```
DS2 - (D (AMOUNT-OF (C-S PRODUCT FURNACE)))
DS2 - (D (AMOUNT-OF (C-S REACTANTS FURNACE)))
DS2 - (D (AMOUNT-OF (C-S OFF-GAS FURNACE)))
DS2 - (D (AMOUNT-OF (C-S REACTANTS BIN)))
DS2 - (D (AMOUNT-OF (C-S OFF-GAS OFFTAKE)))

 (D (TEMP (C-S REACTANTS BIN))): +
 (D (TEMP HEATER)): zero
 (D (AMOUNT-OF (C-S REACTANTS BIN))): -
 (D (PRESSURE (C-S REACTANTS BIN))): -
 (D (TEMP (C-S PRODUCT FURNACE))): -
 (D (FLOW-RATE (HEAT-FLOW))): +
 (D (TEMP (C-S OFF-GAS FURNACE))): -
 (D (AMOUNT-OF (C-S PRODUCT FURNACE))): +
 (D (PRESSURE (C-S PRODUCT FURNACE))): +
 (D (AMOUNT-OF (C-S REACTANTS FURNACE))): -
 (D (PRESSURE (C-S REACTANTS FURNACE))): -
 (D (FLOW-RATE (MATERIAL-FLOW (C-S REACTANTS BIN)))): +
 (D (TEMP-GAINED (COUNTERCURRENT-HEAT-FLOW))): -
 (D (TEMP (C-S REACTANTS FURNACE))): +
 (D (G-RATE (REACTION))): +
 (D (EQ-AMOUNT-OF (C-S REACTANTS FURNACE))): -
 (D (EQ-TEMP (C-S PRODUCT FURNACE))): -
 (D (AMOUNT-OF (C-S OFF-GAS FURNACE))): +
 (D (PRESSURE (C-S OFF-GAS FURNACE))): +
 (D (AMOUNT-OF-IN OFF-GAS FURNACE)): +
 (D (AMOUNT-OF (C-S OFF-GAS OFFTAKE))): +
 (D (PRESSURE (C-S OFF-GAS OFFTAKE))): +
 (D (FLOW-RATE (MATerialL-FLOW (C-S OFF-GAS FURNACE)))): +
 (D (EQ-PRESSURE (C-S OFF-GAS FURNACE))): +
 (D (TEMP-LOST (COUNTERCURRENT-HEAT-FLOW))): -
 (D (TEMP (C-S OFF-GAS OFFTAKE))): +
 (D (AMOUNT-OF-IN OFF-GAS OFFTAKE)): +
 (D (REACTION-TEMP REACTANTS)): zero
```

FIGURE 9.7. Results of Extended QPA on Reactant Temp Increase

Parameter	QPA Heater	EQPA Heater	QPA Reactants	EQPA Reactants
P (reactants bin)	–	–	?	–
A (reactants bin)	–	–	?	–
T (reactants bin)	0	0	+	+
P (reactants furnace)	–	–	?	–
A (reactants furnace)	–	–	?	–
T (reactants furnace)	+	+	?	+
P (product furnace)	+	+	?	+
A (product furnace)	+	+	?	+
T (product furnace)	+	+	?	–
P (off-gas furnace)	+	+	?	+
A (off-gas furnace)	+	+	?	+
T (off-gas furnace)	+	+	?	–
P (off-gas offtake)	+	+	?	+
A (off-gas offtake)	+	+	?	+
T (off-gas offtake)	?	+	+	+
Temperature (htr)	+	+	0	0
Flow-Rate (reactants)	+	+	?	+
Flow-Rate (off-gas)	+	+	?	+
Flow-rate (heat)	+	+	+	+
G-Rate (reaction)	+	+	?	+
Temperature-Lost	?	?	–	–
Temperature-Gained	+	+	–	–

FIGURE 9.8. Extended QPA Example Summary

9.3 Linguistic Perturbation Analysis

QP theory is limited in the range of "what if" or small-signal perturbation analysis questions it can answer by its restricted representations. We have seen that we can reduce the ambiguity in its analyses by adding additional functional characterizations and providing a semiquantitative extension representation for influence magnitudes. In traditional small-signal analysis we can obtain an estimate of the final value of a target parameter by adding the computed delta to the initial value for the parameter. QP theory provides no representation for parameter magnitudes to which we can add a computed delta to obtain any meaningful result. The problem, as we reviewed earlier, is that there is no information within the theory itself that permits us to establish any relevant distinctions between possible parameter values beyond those already made in the quantity space, and these distinctions establish an ordinal, not a cardinal, scale. We can do more in reasoning about the consequences of change by providing an extension theory that can represent distinctions relevant to an *external agent*. Recall that a linguistic variable representation satisfies this requirement. We have already shown, in Chapter 7, how linguistic magnitude information can be incorporated into the quantity spaces of QP theory.

Using linguistic variables as the needed quantitative representation of parameter magnitudes, we have developed a four-step procedure to perform a linguistic version of perturbation analysis. This procedure will need substantial amounts of situation-specific quantitative information, which can be obtained either by default, by observation, or directly from the user. The procedure assumes that we are performing the perturbation analysis around some state for which we know the quantitative extension base values for both the source and target parameters. If we have not been able to establish these values, either by observation or by influence resolution, then we assume that the extension base values are established by a correspondence provided to the system. The four steps are listed below and detailed in subsequent paragraphs:

1. Compute input influence.
2. Propagate influence through influence graph.
3. Convert computed influence into new target parameter value.
4. Check reasonableness of result.

For the purpose of illustration, we shall follow the problem of estimating the effect on reaction rate and off-gas exit temperature if we increase the temperature of the heat source from low to medium. We assume that the extension base values are provided from observation. Computing the input influence is a knowledge-based process. We assume that the system has available a mapping function (parameter specific) that maps from an old and new input parameter value pair to an influence strength.[3] This mapping function can be expressed as a fuzzy relation between input values and influence magnitudes. Given a matrix IR specifying this mapping function, we can compute the influence equivalent of the delta as

$$\begin{aligned} Influence &= Newvalue * Currentvalue * InfluenceRelation \\ \mu_{Iv}(k) &= \vee_{i,j}\mu_{new}(i) \wedge \mu_{old}(j) \wedge \mu_{IR}(i,j,k) \end{aligned}$$

Propagating this influence through the view and process structure of the state uses the extended perturbation analysis algorithm described earlier. The coarseness of the influence representation needed is, in general, a function of the coarseness of the discretization of the goal parameter as well as the number of influence annotations made and their coarseness. We provide no procedure for computing this, but assume the user has selected an appropriate discretization. In general this must be maintained as relatively coarse - as it gets finer and finer, it approaches assuming a linear model, which is an invalid assumption in most cases (see the previous section for further discussion of this point). One problem arises, however, in using the extended qualitative perturbation analysis algorithm to estimate quantitative changes. Influence relations ($I+/I-$) are qualitative abstractions of equations with a temporal aspect. In general, in order to obtain a quantitative estimate of the effect of propagating a delta through a direct influence, we must know how long the delta is in effect. Consider the following examples. Suppose

$$X = -3Y$$

Differentiating this with respect to Y, we obtain

$$\frac{dX}{dt} = -3\frac{dY}{dt}$$

We can represent this qualitatively as

$$(XQ - Y)$$

and the extended qualitative perturbation analysis algorithm we have developed provides correct quantitative, as well as qualitative, results. Consider, however, the case of

$$X = \int Y dt$$

[3] A temperature increase from 90 degrees C to 110 degrees C might be a big or little change - there is no information internal to the theory that can be used to determine this. Since all parameters in a quantity space share a single value discretization, the number of discrete steps in the change does not directly provide this information.

In QP theory this is represented qualitatively as

$$(X\,I+\,Y)$$

However, $dX = Ydt$ We could ignore the meaning of the dt term in the qualitative analysis for three reasons:

1. dt is simply a scaling parameter that affects all direct influences proportionately and therefore does not affect their relative magnitudes when conflicting direct influences are combined.
2. Most directly influenced variables, as we have seen in the preceding chapter, exist in feedback loops that control their values. When considering only the change in equilibrium due to a control action, it is no longer necessary to consider time. The amount of the shift in the equilibrium value is determined solely by the relative strengths of the direct and indirect influences in the feedback loops around the equilibrium variable.
3. When combining direct and indirect influences for a parameter not in equilibrium, we can assume that the strength annotation on a direct influence is chosen to reflect its effect after some nominal time period.

The first and second of these three assumptions are still valid for quantitative (linguistic) analysis, but the third might not be. The extended qualitative perturbation analysis algorithm presented earlier must therefore be extended to scale influences propagated through direct influence arcs ($I+/I-$) by a user-specified time delta. However, in accordance with assumption 2 above, this must only be done for influences that are not part of feedback loops for variables in equilibrium. The examples presented later do not incorporate this extension and must be viewed as estimating results for some standard nominal time delay after the change action is taken (all of the variables of interest are in feedback loops, so this assumption is unnecessary for the parameters shown in Fig. 9.9).

The next step is the inverse of the first step, combining the resulting influence with the initial goal parameter value to obtain a final result. Assuming the influence relation (IR) is represented in matrix form, this inverse relation is straightforward to compute:

$$\mu_{new}(i) = \vee_{j,k}\mu_{influence}(k) \wedge \mu_{old}(k) \wedge \mu_{IR}(i,j,k)$$

Such approximations are subject to substantial inaccuracy, and a person who attempts such rough estimates will try to verify their reasonableness. We can do this by testing whether the results satisfy the quantity restrictions for the state.[4]

[4]This assumes the input change does not result in transition to a qualitatively

We can perform the reasonableness test in either of two ways. First, we can directly test whether or not the estimated value for the target parameter is within its quantity restriction. This can be done using the containment test discussed in Chapter 7. In the following expressions, $QR(x)$ refers to the derived quantity restriction for parameter x in the state under consideration, given those observations that have been made and the quantity conditions imposed by the state. $EV(x)$ is the estimated value of parameter x computed using linguistic perturbation analysis. The direct test between the estimated value and the quantity restriction can then be written as:

$$Contains(QR(x), EV(x))?$$

e.g.

$$Contains(QR(grate), \{[0,1]/125 + [0,1]/150 + [0,1]/175\})?$$

Alternatively, a more extensive test can be performed by estimating the final values of all parameters of the state and testing whether or not all parameter pairs satisfy all quantity conditions imposed on them by the state:

$$(EV(x)\, R\, EV(y))?$$

for all R in the quantity conditions for the state.

9.4 LPA Extended Example

This section contains computer output for an extended example of what happens to four critical parameters within the furnace when we increase the temperature of the heat source from low to moderate. The results are presented in a summarized form in Fig. 9.9. Notice that the results make several significant quantitative distinctions, such as the fact that, whereas the temperature of the product in the furnace will change only slightly, if at all, the off-gas exit temperature may increase significantly.

9.4.1 Input Script

```
;;;
;;;  define various delta to influence conversion scales
;;;  ''imp'' and ''imp-10''
;;;
(deffact '(QDelta-I-table (temp heater) ...))
```

different state. The situation in which the change causes transition to a qualitatively different state is a different problem, one that is addressed in QP theory by differential qualitative (DQ) analysis.

```
{\it Values prior to control action}:

(Temp heater):    {[1,  1]/2500}

(Temp product):   {[0, 0.01]/1000 + [.84, 1]/1500
                    + [0, .01]/2000}

G-Rate:           {[.96, 1]/125 + [.36, 1]/150\

(Temp (c-s off-gas offtake)): {[.96, 1]/200 + [.36, 1]/300}


{\it Now do LPA - new heater temp is one discretization}
 {\it element higher than before}:

(lpa h new-value = {[1, 1]/3000})

{\it Estimates following control action}:

(Temp heater): {[1, 1]/3000}

(Temp product):
   {[0, .01]/1000 + [0, 0]/1500 + [0, 0]/2000 + [0, .01]/2500}

G-rate:          {[0, 1]/125 + [0, 1]/150 + [0, 1]/175}

(Temp (c-s off-gas offtake):
      {[0, 1]/100 + [0, 1]/200 + [0, 1]/300 + [0, 1]/400}
```

FIGURE 9.9. Linguistic Perturbation Analysis Example

```
(deffact '(QDelta-I-table (temp (c-s product furnace)) ...))
(deffact '(QDelta-I-table (temp (c-s reactants bin)) ...))
(deffact '(QDelta-I-Table (temp (c-s off-gas offtake)) ...))
(deffact '(QDelta-I-Table g-rate ...))

;;; identify the quantity spaces and establish discretizations
;;; for each one relevant to this problem

(build-q-spaces)

;;; temp q-space - first four are reactants in bin, next four
;;; are product and off-gas in furnace, last four (two overlap)
;;; are heater temp

(set-q-space-scale
   'q-space16 '(50 100 150 200 1000 1500 2000 2500 3000 3500))

;;; generation-rate

(set-q-space-scale 'q-space4 '(100 125 150 175 200))

;;; off-gas in offtake

(set-q-space-scale 'q-space5 '(100 200 300 400 500))

;;;   establish initial values for important quantities

(defQuantityValue '(temp heater)
  '([0, 1] [0, 1] [0, 1] [0, 1] [0, 1] [0, 1] [0, 1] [1, 0]
             [0, 1] [0, 1]))
(defquantityvalue '(temp (c-s product furnace))
    '([0, 1] [0, 1] [0, 1] [0, 1] [.2, 1]
     [.6, 0] [.2, 1] [0, 1]  [0, 1] [0, 1]))
(defquantityvalue '(temp (c-s reactants bin))
  '([0, 1] [1, 0] [0, 1] [0, 1] [0, 1]
    [0, 1] [0, 1] [0, 1]  [0, 1] [0, 1]))
(defquantityvalue '(temp (c-s off-gas offtake))
  '([0, 1] [.8, 0] [.2, 0] [0, 1] [0, 1]))
(defquantityvalue 'g-rate
      '([0, 1] [.8, 0.] [.2, 0] [0, 1] [0, 1]))

;;;  do influence resolution to establish needed annotations

(influence-resolution env)
```

```
;;;   show initial values in output

(get-quantity-value (temp heater))
(get-quantity-value (temp (c-s product furnace)))
(get-quantity-value (temp (c-s reactants bin)))
(get-quantity-value g-rate)
(get-quantity-value (temp (c-s off-gas offtake)))

;;;   now actually do Linguistic Perturbation Analysis

(lpa (temp heater) '(no no no no no no no no yes no) env)

;;;   display results

(lpa-value (temp heater))
(lpa-value (temp (c-s product furnace)))
(lpa-value (temp (c-s reactants bin)))
(lpa-value g-rate)
(lpa-value (temp (c-s off-gas offtake)))
```

9.4.2 Output Trace

The following is the output trace from the above script:

```
;;;   Q-Spaces found

Q-space26:  (QUALITY (C-S REACTANTS FURNACE))
Q-space25:  (REACTION-TEMP REACTANTS)
Q-space24:  (PRESSURE (C-S OFF-GAS OFFTAKE))
            (PRESSURE (C-S OFF-GAS FURNACE))
Q-space23:  (AMOUNT-OF-IN OFF-GAS FURNACE)
            (AMOUNT-OF (C-S OFF-GAS FURNACE))
Q-space22:  (PRESSURE (C-S REACTANTS FURNACE))
            (PRESSURE (C-S REACTANTS BIN))
Q-space21:  (AMOUNT-OF-IN REACTANTS BIN)
            (AMOUNT-OF (C-S REACTANTS BIN))
Q-space20:  (AMOUNT-OF-IN REACTANTS FURNACE)
            (AMOUNT-OF (C-S REACTANTS FURNACE))
Q-space19:  (PRESSURE (C-S PRODUCT FURNACE))
Q-space18:  (AMOUNT-OF-IN PRODUCT FURNACE)
            (AMOUNT-OF (C-S PRODUCT FURNACE))
Q-space16:  (TEMP (C-S REACTANTS BIN))
            (TEMP (C-S OFF-GAS FURNACE))
            (TEMP (C-S PRODUCT FURNACE))
```

```
            (TEMP HEATER)
Q-space15:  (FLOW-RATE (MATERIAL-FLOW (C-S REACTANTS BIN)))
Q-space14:  (FLOW-RATE (MATERIAL-FLOW (C-S OFF-GAS FURNACE)))
Q-space13:  (AMOUNT-OF-IN OFF-GAS OFFTAKE)
            (AMOUNT-OF (C-S OFF-GAS OFFTAKE))
Q-space10:  (TEMP (C-S REACTANTS FURNACE))
Q-space7:  (FLOW-RATE HEAT-FLOW)
Q-space5:  (TEMP (C-S OFF-GAS OFFTAKE))
Q-space4:  (G-RATE REACTION)
Q-space2:  TEMP-GAINED
Q-space1:  TEMP-LOST

;;;  influence resolution annotation output

Ambiguities detected - Attempt to annotate?(Y or N) YES

Possible equilibrium for: (TEMP (C-S PRODUCT FURNACE))
 Due to action of:   (FLOW-RATE HEAT-FLOW), G-RATE
 Create equilibrium value?(Y or N) YES
 Assume equilibrium?(Y or N) YES
 Annotate paths?(Y or N) YES
  Can you annotate ((TEMP (C-S PRODUCT FURNACE))
                   Q+ (HEAT (C-S PRODUCT FURNACE)))? NO
  Can you annotate ((HEAT (C-S PRODUCT FURNACE))
                   I+ (FLOW-RATE HEAT-FLOW))? YES
   Globally?(Y or N) YES
    Enter annotation: 'WEAK +'
  Can you annotate ((FLOW-RATE HEAT-FLOW))
                   Q- (TEMP (C-S PRODUCT FURNACE)) ? NO
  Can you annotate ((TEMP (C-S PRODUCT FURNACE))
                   Q+ (HEAT (C-S PRODUCT FURNACE)))? NO
  Can you annotate ((HEAT (C-S PRODUCT FURNACE))
                   I- G-RATE) ? YES
    Globally?(Y or N) YES
     Enter annotation: 'STRONG +'
  Can you annotate
   (G-RATE  Q+ (TEMP (C-S PRODUCT FURNACE))) ? NO

Possible equilibrium for: (AMOUNT-OF (C-S REACTANTS FURNACE))
 Due to action of:
  (FLOW-RATE (MATERIAL-FLOW (C-S REACTANTS BIN))), G-RATE
 Create equilibrium value?(Y or N) YES.
 Assume equilibrium?(Y or N) YES.
 Annotate paths?(Y or N) NO.
```

```
Possible equilibrium for: (TEMP (C-S PRODUCT FURNACE))
 Due to action of: (FLOW-RATE HEAT-FLOW), G-RATE
 Create equilibrium value?(Y or N) NO
 Annotate paths?(Y or N) NO.

Possible equilibrium for: (PRESSURE (C-S OFF-GAS FURNACE))
 Due to action of:
  G-RATE, (FLOW-RATE (MATERIAL-FLOW (C-S OFF-GAS FURNACE)))
 Create equilibrium value?(Y or N) YES.
 Assume equilibrium?(Y or N) YES.
 Annotate paths?(Y or N) NO.

;;; show initial values before lpa analysis

(temp heater):
  ([0, 1] [0, 1] [0, 1] [0, 1] [0, 1] [0, 1] [0, 1] [1, 0]
   [0, 1] [0, 1])
(temp (c-s product furnace)):
  ([0, 1] [0, 1] [0, 1] [0, 1] [0, 0.99] [0.84, 0]
   [0, 0.99] [0, 1] [0, 1] [0, 1])
(temp (c-s reactants bin)):
 ([0, 1] [1, 0] [0, 1] [0, 1] [0, 1] [0, 1] [0, 1] [0, 1]
  [0, 1] [0, 1])
g-rate: ([0, 1] [0.96, 0] [0.36, 0] [0, 1] [0, 1])
(temp (c-s off-gas offtake)):
  ([0, 1] [0.96, 0] [0.36, 0] [0, 1] [0, 1])

;;; now do LPA - note new heater temp is one discretization
;;; element higher than before

(lpa (temp heater))
    '(no no no no no no no no yes no) env)}

;;;   Linguistic Perturbation analysis output

(temp heater):
 ([0, 1] [0, 1] [0, 1] [0, 1] [0, 1] [0, 1] [0, 1]
  [0, 1] [1, 0] [0, 1])
(temp (c-s product furnace)):
 ([0, 1] [0, 1] [0, 1] [0, 1] [0, 0.99] [0, 5.96e-8]
  [0, 5.96e-8] [0, 0.99] [0, 1] [0, 1])
(temp (c-s reactants bin)):
 ([0, 1] [1, 0] [0, 1] [0, 1] [0, 1] [0, 1] [0, 1] [0, 1]
  [0, 1] [0, 1] [0, 1])
g-rate:  ([0, 1] [0, 0] [0, 0] [0, 0] [0, 1])
```

```
(temp (c-s off-gas offtake)):
  ([0, 0] [0, 0] [0, 0] [0, 0] [0, 1])


;;;   EQPA output generated from invocation of EQPA by
;;;    Linguistic Perturbation Analysis

 ((D (TEMP HEATER)) . \#<INFLUENCE 11057462>): ' weak + '
DS2 - (D (AMOUNT-OF (C-S OFF-GAS FURNACE)))
DS2 - (D (AMOUNT-OF (C-S PRODUCT FURNACE)))
DS2 - (D (AMOUNT-OF (C-S REACTANTS FURNACE)))
DS2 - (D (AMOUNT-OF (C-S OFF-GAS OFFTAKE)))
DS2 - (D (AMOUNT-OF (C-S REACTANTS BIN)))

Ambiguities detected - Attempt to annotate?(Y or N) NO
 (D (TEMP (C-S REACTANTS BIN))): 0
 (D (TEMP HEATER)):  weak +
 (D (AMOUNT-OF (C-S REACTANTS BIN))): weak -
 (D (PRESSURE (C-S REACTANTS BIN))): weak -
 (D (AMOUNT-OF-IN REACTANTS BIN)): weak -
 (D (TEMP (C-S PRODUCT FURNACE))): 0  weak +
 (D (FLOW-RATE HEAT-FLOW)):  weak +
 (D (TEMP (C-S OFF-GAS FURNACE))): 0  weak +
 (D (AMOUNT-OF (C-S PRODUCT FURNACE))): 0  weak +
 (D (PRESSURE (C-S PRODUCT FURNACE))): 0  weak +
 (D (AMOUNT-OF-IN PRODUCT FURNACE)): 0  weak +
 (D (AMOUNT-OF (C-S REACTANTS FURNACE))): weak -
 (D (PRESSURE (C-S REACTANTS FURNACE))): weak -
 (D (FLOW-RATE (MATERIAL-FLOW
                 (C-S REACTANTS BIN)))): 0 - weak +
 (D (TEMP-GAINED )): 0  weak +
 (D (TEMP (C-S REACTANTS FURNACE))): 0  weak +
 (D (G-RATE )): 0  weak +
 (D (EQ-AMOUNT-OF (C-S REACTANTS FURNACE))): weak -
 (D (EQ-TEMP (C-S PRODUCT FURNACE))):  weak +
 (D (AMOUNT-OF-IN REACTANTS FURNACE)): weak -
 (D (AMOUNT-OF (C-S OFF-GAS FURNACE))): 0  weak +
 (D (PRESSURE (C-S OFF-GAS FURNACE))): 0  weak +
 (D (AMOUNT-OF-IN OFF-GAS FURNACE)): 0  weak +
 (D (AMOUNT-OF (C-S OFF-GAS OFFTAKE))): 0  weak +
 (D (PRESSURE (C-S OFF-GAS OFFTAKE))): 0  weak +
 (D (FLOW-RATE (MATERIAL-FLOW (C-S OFF-GAS FURNACE)))):
                                              0  weak +
 (D (EQ-PRESSURE (C-S OFF-GAS FURNACE))): 0
 (D (TEMP-LOST )): weak -  weak +
```

```
(D (TEMP (C-S OFF-GAS OFFTAKE))): weak -  weak +
(D (AMOUNT-OF-IN OFF-GAS OFFTAKE)): 0  weak +
(D (REACTION-TEMP REACTANTS)): 0
```

9.5 Summary

In this chapter we have developed a technique for using QP theory to reason about the consequences of continuous control actions within a qualitative state. Starting from the classical method of small-signal analysis, we developed a qualitative notion of small-signal analysis and extended the basic influence resolution algorithm of Forbus to perform this analysis. We then combined this basic algorithm with the quantitative extensions for parameter values developed earlier and presented a technique for estimating the effects of continuous control actions within a qualitative state.

10

Evaluation and Conclusion

10.1 Review

We began this work with an interest in pursuing a symbolic, knowledge-based approach to the control of complex engineered systems. The work presented in this thesis has been based on two premises. First, we believe that qualitative process (QP) theory offers potential for reasoning about the control of complex engineered physical systems, especially when they are poorly understood or the capability for making observations of the systems is limited. Second, we surmise that problem solving in this domain proceeds by an iterative process of building, applying, and patching models of the system under consideration.

On the basis of these premises we examined QP theory and found it severely limited in its present form. First, it is often unable to determine unambiguously the qualitative value of system parameters. Often, when information that could potentially serve to disambiguate results is available, there is no way to express the information within QP theory. Second, QP theory in its current form provides no facility for performing quantitative reasoning. Many of the tasks involved in control of engineered systems involve adjustments of continuous control parameters or estimation of effects relative to some scale external to the system under consideration. Both of these reasoning tasks require some form of quantitative capability.

In order to surmount these problems, we developed a set of extensions to QP theory which reduce internal ambiguity resulting from inability to resolve conflicting influences and expand the scope of QP theory by providing an extension theory that can reason semiquantitatively about consequences of external control actions. These extensions are based on the use of linguistic variables to represent the uncertain or imprecise system-specific information typically available to supplement models built from a domain theory. The extension set has three basic components:

1. A *linguistic quantity space*, which can represent partial information about quantity conditions and relate quantity orderings with linguistic descriptions of parameter magnitudes. These linguistic parameter values make user-relevant distinctions.

2. *Linguistic functional strength annotations* and an extension to the influence resolution algorithm that makes use of these annotations to resolve ambiguity.

3. *Linguistic perturbation* analysis, which builds on all of the above mechanisms and provides a way to estimate the effects of hypothetical control actions.

We have shown, at least for the example problem considered in this thesis, that these extensions can be used to derive answers to several qualitative and quantitative questions that cannot be answered using basic QP theory. Specifically, we have demonstrated:

- The estimation of likelihoods for various system states, given approximate and uncertain sensor information (*linguistic measurement interpretation*).
- The unambiguous determination of qualitative parameter values, given linguistic functional strength characterizations (*linguistic influence resolution*).
- The quantitative estimation of the effects of adjustments to continuous control parameters (*linguistic perturbation analysis*).

10.2 Evaluation

Each of the above three algorithms requires different information from the user and makes certain assumptions about the information provided that might limit the applicability of the algorithm. Linguistic measurement interpretation is the most general and assumption-free of the three. The only assumption made is that each of the measurements provided is made independently of the others. If this is not the case, the dependence can be explicitly represented as a justification network external to the QP model under consideration.

Linguistic influence resolution (LIR) derives its power from two sources, functional strength annotations and an appropriate discretization of the influence propagation parameter. We have already identified four classes of annotation: universal, system specific, state specific, and query specific. Of these, query-specific annotations are potentially the most troubling. Although we have specifically excluded from consideration in this thesis the source of annotation information, it still remains to be demonstrated that it is at least feasible that some external knowledge source could provide the required information. Recognizing that an annotation is appropriate requires that sufficient information be available at the time the annotation is requested. A query-specific annotation is requested when preliminary application of the LIR algorithm reveals an ambiguity in the result for some interesting parameter. At that time, several facts are available to aid the search for relevant query-specific annotations:

1. The subgraph causing the ambiguity can be recognized using the graph-matching techniques sketched here.

2. The entry point of the change into the graph is readily identifiable by examining the change values of the nodes influencing subgraph nodes.

3. The component(s) that generated the subgraph can be identified as long as this information is recorded when the influence graph is constructed (the current implementation does not do this).

These facts seem to be exactly those that might be expected to trigger recognition of the relevant query-specific patch.

The second problem is the choice of an appropriate discretization for the influence parameter. This has been discussed earlier and shown not to be as critical as it might seem. The worst result of choosing too coarse a discretization is that some ambiguity remains that might have been able to be eliminated from the final result. Also, a discretization finer than that of the control and observable variable values is only necessary when combining annotated influences, not when computing individual annotated influences. Thus, the minimum discretization needed to maintain full information grows more slowly than might be expected. We have obtained adequate results for the example used in this thesis by using an influence discretization with the same coarseness as the discretization for functional strength annotations.

Finally, we note an implicit assumption that annotations are intended to resolve local ambiguities. There may be a danger when an influence computed using a strength annotation propagates outside the locale where it is valid and combines with an influence from another unrelated annotation. It is partially for this reason that we have adopted the approach of only adding those annotations actually needed to resolve ambiguity, rather than all possible annotations. This procedure has been sufficient for all examples studied so far. Should it turn out inadequate in other applications, another alternative would be to "age" influences, that is, to broaden or fuzzify them at each propagation step. This would serve to nullify the effect of strength annotations outside the immediate environment for which they are intended.

The last and most complex of the procedures we have described is linguistic perturbation analysis(LPA). It depends on the ability of the user to establish suitable discretizations for parameters of interest, in addition to all of the information needed for linguistic influence resolution. It also places special demands on the functional annotations. These annotations must now describe quantized partial sensitivities of one parameter with respect to another. Although this use of annotations is consistent with the use made by linguistic influence resolution (and in fact solves the problems created by propagation beyond local domain of applicability described above), it makes far more intensive use of the annotation mechanism. This, therefore, raises again, and even more strongly, the problem of establishing an appropriate discretization for the influence parameter. However, the same comments made earlier apply here - the only danger from an insufficient discretization is an increase in the ambiguity of the result. In fact, establishing a fairly coarse discretization can be a useful way to prevent "overlinearization" of the model. That is, it prevents the derivation of results that are critically dependent on the linearity assumption inherent in LPA. Our development of the LPA algorithm depended on equilibrium assumptions. An extension of this to nonequilibrium situations is necessary. Finally, it is not yet clear that the use of the same annotations is valid when a direct influence is used to estimate a second derivative in the basic QPA algorithm.

10.3 Further Research

The research described here, as is often the case, is only a beginning, and much work remains to be done. Most important, the work described here must be extended to include limit analysis, the fourth basic deduction in QP theory. With semiquantitative estimates of both parameter values and change rates, it should be possible to choose between possible future states that basic QP theory cannot disambiguate, as well as estimate state durations.

Also, we have given only the briefest sketch of possible kinds of additional functional descriptions that could be used to reduce the ambiguity of the results of the basic QP theory deductions. We have been unsuccessful in formulating a QP model that predicts that a fluid flow into a container already containing some fluid, where the temperature is the same everywhere, does not change the temperature of the fluid in the container. There is some basic aspect of the functional relationships involved that cannot be represented with the partial functional representation provided. Also, functional relationships often have a temporal character as well as relative strengths. What characteristics of relationships between continuous parameters of a situation do people observe? How are these characteristics remembered, and how are they used in problem solving?

This last question touches on another major research area, the subject of our second basic premise. What is the nature of the overall problem-solving architecture? What other kinds of knowledge are available during reasoning about physical systems besides domain theories of the kind representable in QP theory? How are they combined? We have suggested ambiguity-based model patching as one possible mechanism for interaction of different kinds of knowledge - there must be others.

10.4 Conclusion

We have presented a sketch of an extension to QP theory that reduces the ambiguity inherent in qualitative reasoning, while retaining the advantages this technique offers. This extension replaces the qualitative quantity space used by Forbus with a linguistic quantity space and, additionally, permits the user to specify linguistically the strength of functional relationships between variables and linguistically characterize variable values. We have demonstrated that these extensions directly address the sources of ambiguity within QP theory, and we have discussed further research on these issues.

10.5 References

[AR86] A. Agogino and A. Rege. Ides: Influence diagram based expert system. In X. Avula et al, editor, *Mathematical Modelling in Science and Technology*. Pergamon Press, Elmsford, N.Y., 1986.

[Axe76] R. Axelrod. *Structure of Decision: The Cognitive Maps of the Political Elites*. Princeton University Press, Princeton, N.J., 1976.

[Bal81] J. Baldwin. An automated fuzzy knowledge base. In R. Yager, editor, *Fuzzy Systems*. Pergamon Press, Elmsford, N.Y., 1981.

[Bal85a] J. Baldwin. Support logic programming. Technical Report ITRC 65, Information Technology Research Center, Univ. of Bristol, U.K., 1985.

[Bal85b] J. F. Baldwin. Fuzzy sets and expert systems. *Inf. Sci.*, 36:123–156, 1985.

[Bar81] J. Barnett. Computational methods for a mathematical theory of evidence. In *Proceedings of IJCAI-81*, pages 868–875. International Joint Conference on Artificial Intelligence, Aug. 1981.

[BS84] B. Buchanan and E. Shortliffe. *Rule-Based Expert Systems: The Mycin Experiments of the Stanford Heuristic Programming Project*. Addison-Wesley, Reading, Mass., 1984.

[Bun78] A. Bundy. Will it reach the top? prediction in the mechanics world. *Artif. Intell.*, 10(1):129–147, 1978.

[BW81] A. Bundy and B. Welham. Using meta-level inference for selective application of multiple rewrite rule sets in algebraic manipulation. *Artif. Intell.*, 16(2):189–212, 1981.

[BZ82] J. Baldwin and S. Zhou. A fuzzy relational inference language. *Fuzzy Sets Sys.*, 14, 1982.

[Che85] P. Cheeseman. In defense of probability. In *Proceedings of the 9th IJCAI*, pages 1002–1009. International Joint Conference on Artificial Intelligence, August 1985.

[Coc80] I. Cochin. *Analysis and Design of Dynamic Systems*. Harper and Row, New York, 1980.

[Coh84] P. Cohen. *Heuristic Reasoning about Uncertainty: An Artificial Intelligence Approach*. Pitman, London, 1984.

[D'A84] B. D'Ambrosio. Fm - an object oriented expert programming system for experiments in approximate reasoning. Master's thesis, University of California, Berkeley, Apr. 1984.

[D'A85] B. D'Ambrosio et al. Levels of abstraction in model-based reasoning. In *Proceedings of ROBEXS '85*, pages 19–22. Robotics and Expert Systems Division, Instrument Society of America, June 1985.

[D'A86] B. D'Ambrosio. *Qualitative process theory using linguistic variables.* PhD thesis, University of California, Berkeley, December 1986.

[D'A88a] Bruce D. D'Ambrosio. A hybrid approach to management of uncertainty. *International Journal of Approximate Reasoning*, 2(1), February 1988.

[D'A88b] Bruce D. D'Ambrosio. Process, structure, and modularity in reasoning under uncertainty. In *Proceedings of the 1987 Workshop on Uncertainty in AI*, pages 64–72. American Association for Artificial Intelligence, August 1988.

[dK77] J. de Kleer. Multiple representations of knowledge in a mechanics problem-solver. In *Proceedings of the 5th IJCAI*, pages 299–304. International Joint Conference on Artificial Intelligence, August 1977.

[dK79] J. de Kleer. Causal and teleological reasoning in circuit recognition. Technical Report TR-529, Artificial Intelligence Laboratory, Massachusetts Institute of Technology., Sept. 1979.

[dK86a] J. de Kleer. An assumption-based tms. *Artif. Intell.*, 28(2):127–162, Mar. 1986.

[dK86b] J. de Kleer. Extending the atms. *Artif. Intell.*, 28(2):163–196, Mar. 1986.

[dK86c] J. de Kleer. Problem-solving with the atms. *Artif. Intell.*, 28(2):197–224, Mar. 1986.

[dKB84a] J. de Kleer and D. Bobrow. Qualitative reasoning with higher-order derivatives. In *Proceedings National Conference on Artificial Intelligence.* American Association for Artificial Intelligence, Aug. 1984.

[dKB84b] J. de Kleer and J. Brown. A qualitative physics based on confluences. *Artif. Intell.*, 24(1-3):7–83, December 1984.

[dKW87] J. de Kleer and B. Williams. Diagnosing multiple faults. *Artif. Intell.*, 32(1):97–131, Apr. 1987.

[Doy79] J. Doyle. A truth maintenance system. *Artificial Intelligence*, 12(3):231–272, 1979.

[ET82] J. Estathiou and R. Tong. Ranking fuzzy sets: A decision theoretic approach. *IEEE Trans. on Sys., Man, Cybern.*, SMC-12(5):655–659, Sept.-Oct. 1982.

[FN71] R. Fikes and N. Nilsson. Strips: A new approach to the application of theorem proving to problem solving. *Artif. Intell.*, 2:189–208, 1971.

[For84] K. Forbus. *Qualitative process theory.* PhD thesis, Massachusetts Institute of Technology, Cambridge, Mass., July 1984.

[GS85] J. Gordon and E. Shortliffe. A method for managing evidential reasoning in a hierarchical hypothesis space. *Artif. Intell.*, 26(3):323–358, July 1985.

[Han87] Steve Hanks. Temporal reasoning about uncertain worlds. In *Proceedings of the 3rd Workshop on Uncertainty in AI*, pages 114–123. American Association for Artificial Intelligence, August 1987.

[Hay71] P. Hayes. The frame problem and related problems in artificial intelligence. In Michie, editor, *Machine Intelligence 6*, pages 45–59. American Elsevier, New York, 1971.

[Hay79a] P. Hayes. Naive physics 1 - ontology for liquids. Memo, Centre pour les etudes Semantiques et Cognitives, Geneva, 1979.

[Hay79b] P. Hayes. The naive physics manifesto. In D. Michie, editor, *Expert Systems in the Micro-Electronic Age.* Edinburgh University Press, Edinburgh, Scotland, 1979.

[HH87] D. Heckerman and E. Horvitz. On the expressiveness of rule-based systems for reasoning with uncertainty. In *Proceedings of AAAI87*, pages 121–126. American Association for Artificial Intelligence, August 1987.

[HM69] P. Hayes and J. McCarthy. Some philosophical problems from the standpoint of artificial intelligence. In Meltzer and Michie, editors, *Machine Intelligence 4*, pages 463–504. American Elsevier, New York, 1969.

[HM84] R. Howard and J. Matheson. Influence diagrams. In Howard and Matheson, editors, *The Principles and Applications of Decision Analysis.* Addison-Wesley, Menlo Park, Calif., 1984.

[HO82] L. Holmblad and J. Ostergaard. Control of a cement kiln by fuzzy logic. In M. Gupta and E. Sanchez, editors, *Fuzzy Information and Decision Processes.* North Holland, 1982.

[Kos86] B. Kosko. Fuzzy cognitive maps. *Int. J. Man-Mach. Stud.*, 24(1):65–75, January 1986.

[Kui84] B. Kuipers. Commonsense reasoning about causality: Deriving behavior from structure. *Artif. Intell.*, 24(1-3):169–205, December 1984.

[KvNL76] W. Kickert and H. van Nauta Lemke. The application of fuzzy set theory to control a warm water process. *Automatica*, 12(4):301 – 308, 1976.

[Lak72] G. Lakoff. Hedges: A study in meaning criteria and the logic of fuzzy concepts. In *Proceedings of 8th Reg. Meeting of the Chicago Linguistics Society*, Chicago, Ill., Apr. 1972. Univ. of Chicago Linguistics Dept.

[Lar80] P. Larsen. Industrial application of fuzzy logic control. *Int. J. Man-Mach. Stud.*, 12:3–10, 1980.

[Lar85] L. Larkin. A fuzzy logic controller for aircraft flight control. In M. Sugeno, editor, *Industrial Applications of Fuzzy Control*, pages 87–104. Elsevier Science, 1985.

[LeF74] R. LeFaivre. Fuzzy: A programming language for fuzzy problem solving. Tech rep. 202, Univ. of Wisconson, Madison, 1974.

[LG83] J. Lowrance and T. Garvey. Evidential reasoning: An implementation for multisensor integration. Tech Note 307, SRI International, Menlo Park, Ca., Dec. 1983.

[Liu86] G. Liu. Causal and plausible reasoning in expert systems. In *Proceedings of AAAI86*, pages 222–225. American Association for Artificial Intelligence, 1986.

[LL88] Kathryn Laskey and Paul Lehner. Belief maintenance: An integrated approach to uncertainty management. In *Proceedings of AAAI88*, pages 210–214. American Association for Artificial Intelligence, August 1988.

[MA75] E. Mamdani and S. Assilian. An experiment in linguistic synthesis with a fuzzy logic controller. *Int. J. of Man Mach. Stud.*, 7:1–13, 1975.

[Mam76] E. Mamdani. Advances in the linguistic synthesis of fuzzy controllers. *Int. Journal of Man Mach. Stud.*, 8:669 – 678, 1976.

[McA80] D. McAllester. An outlook on truth maintenance. AI Memo 551, Artificial Intelligence Laboratory, Massachusetts Institue of Technology, Aug. 1980.

[McA82] D. McAllester. Reasoning utility package user's manual. Memo AI Memo 667, Artificial Intelligence Laboratory, Massachusetts Institue of Technology, Apr. 1982.

[Mil76] A. Miller et al. Development of automated aids for decision analysis. Tech rep., SRI International, Menlo Park, Ca., 1976.

[Moo66] R. Moore. *Interval Analysis.* Prentice-Hall, Englewood Cliffs, N.J., 1966.

[MS83] Joao P. Martins and Stuart C. Shapiro. Reasoning in multiple belief spaces. In *Proceedings of IJCAI83*, pages 370–373. International Joint Conference on Artificial Intelligence, 1983.

[MS85] J. Maiers and Y. Sherif. Applications of fuzzy set theory. *IEEE Trans. Sys., Man, Cybern.*, SMC-15(1):175–189, January/February 1985.

[MS87] Michael L. Mavrovouniotis and George. Stephanopoulos. Reasoning with orders of magnitude and approximate relations. In *Proceedings of AAAI87*, pages 626–630. American Association for Artificial Intelligence, 1987.

[Mur85] Y. Murayama et al. Optimizing control of a diesel engine. In M. Sugeno, editor, *Industrial Applications of Fuzzy Control*, pages 63–72. Elsevier Science, 1985.

[Pan83] Y. Pan. *Qualitative Reasonings with Deep-level Mechanism Models for Diagnoses of Dependent Failures.* PhD thesis, Univ. of Illinois at Urbana Champaign, Dec. 1983.

[Ped85] W. Pedrycz. Design of fuzzy control algorithms with the aid of fuzzy models. In M. Sugeno, editor, *Industrial Applications of Fuzzy Control*, pages 87–104. Elsevier Science, 1985.

[Raj84] R. Rajagopalan. Qualitative modelling in the turbojet engine domain. In *Proceedings AAAI84*, pages 283–287. American Association for Artificial Intelligence, Aug. 1984.

[Rie77] C. Rieger. The declarative representation and procedural simulation of causality in physical mechanisms. In *Proceedings of the 5th IJCAI*, pages 250–255. International Joint Conference on Artificial Intelligence, Aug. 1977.

[Sac85] E. Sacks. Qualitative mathematical reasoning. In *Proceedings of IJCAI-85*, pages 137–139. International Joint Conference on Artificial Intelligence, Aug. 1985.

[Sha76] G. Shafer. *A Mathematical Theory of Evidence.* Princeton University Press, Princeton, N.J., 1976.

[Sim83] R. G. Simmons. Representing and reasoning about change in geologic interpretation. Master's thesis, Artificial Intelligence Laboratory, Massachusetts Institute of Technology, May 1983.

[SS77] R. Stallman and G. Sussman. Forward reasoning and dependency-directed backtracking in a system for computer aided circuit analysis. *Artif. Intell.*, 9:135–196, 1977.

[Ste80] G. Steele. ... *Constraints ...* PhD thesis, Massachusetts Institute of Technology, August 1980. full title begins: A Dissertation on Research Concerning The...

[Ste83] L. Steels. Descriptions as constraints in object oriented representations. In *Proceedings of IJCAI-83*, pages 395–397. International Joint Conference on Artificial Intelligence, Aug. 1983.

[Ton76] R. Tong. Analysis of fuzzy control algorithms using the relation matrix. *Int. J. Man-Mach. Stud.*, 8:679–686, 1976.

[Ton80] R. Tong. Fuzzy control of the activated sludge wastewater treatment process. *Automatica*, 16(6):695–702, 1980.

[Ton84] R. Tong. A retrospective view of fuzzy control systems. *Fuzzy Sets Sys.*, 14:199–210, 1984.

[Ton85] R. Tong. An annotated bibliography of fuzzy control. In M. Sugeno, editor, *Industrial Applications of Fuzzy Control*, pages 249–269. Elsevier Science, 1985.

[Wei84] S. Weiss *et al.* A model-based method for computer-aided medical decision making. In W. Clancey and E. Shortliffe, editors, *Readings in Medical Artificial Intelligence*, chapter 7, pages 160–189. Addison-Wesley, Menlo Park, Calif., 1984.

[Wen75] F. Wenstop. *Application of linguistic variables in the analysis of organizations.* PhD thesis, University of California, Berkeley, 1975.

[Wen80] F. Wenstop. Quantitative analysis with linguistic variables. *Fuzzy Sets Sys.*, 4:99–115, 1980.

[Wil88] B. C. Williams. Minima: A symbolic approach to qualitative algebraic reasoning. In *Proceedings of AAAI-88*, pages 264–269. American Association for Artificial Intelligence, 1988.

[WS83a] T. Whalen and B. Schott. Decision support with fuzzy production systems. In P Wang, editor, *Advances in Fuzzy Set Theory and Applications.* Plenum Press, 1983.

[WS83b] T. Whalen and B. Schott. Representing and manipulating fuzzy knowledge about forecasting problems and techniques. In *Proceedings of the International Conference on Systems, Man, and Cybernetics*, pages 127–131. IEEE, 1983.

[WS85] T. Whalen and B. Schott. Advances in linguistic processing. pages 248 – 253. IEEE, N.Y., 1985.

[Yen85] J. Yen. A model of evidential reasoning in a hierarchical hypothesis space. Tech Rep. UCB/CSD 86/277, Computer Science Division, University of California Berkeley, Dec. 1985.

[YM85] S. Yasunobu and S. Miyamoto. Automatic train operation system. In M. Sugeno, editor, *Industrial Applications of Fuzzy Control*, pages 1–18. Elsevier Science, 1985.

[Zad73] L. Zadeh. Outline of a new approach to the analysis of complex systems and decsion processes. *IEEE Trans. on Sys. Man Cybern.*, 3(1):28–44, 1973.

[Zad75a] L. Zadeh. The concept of a linguistic variable and its application to approximate reasoning - i. *Inf. Sci.*, 8:199–249, 1975.

[Zad75b] L. Zadeh. The concept of a linguistic variable and its application to approximate reasoning - ii. *Inf. Sci.*, 8:301–357, 1975.

[Zad75c] L. Zadeh. The concept of a linguistic variable and its application to approximate reasoning - iii. *Inf. Sci.*, 9:43–80, 1975.

[Zad79] L. Zadeh. A theory of approximate reasoning. In Hayes et al J., editor, *Machine Intelligence 9*, chapter 7, pages 149–193. John Wiley and Sons, Inc., 1979.

[Zad82] L. Zadeh. A computational approach to fuzzy quantifiers in natural languages. Tech. Memo M82/36 (revised), University of California, Berkeley/ERL, May 1982.

[Zad85] L. Zadeh. A simple view of the dempster-shafer theory of evidence and its implications for the rule of combination. Tech Rep. 33, University of California; Berkeley; Institute of Cognitive Studies, Nov. 1985.

Index

MIX
Papier aus verantwortungsvollen Quellen
Paper from responsible sources
FSC® C105338

If you have any concerns about our products,
you can contact us on
ProductSafety@springernature.com

In case Publisher is established outside the EU,
the EU authorized representative is:
Springer Nature Customer Service Center GmbH
Europaplatz 3, 69115 Heidelberg, Germany

Printed by Libri Plureos GmbH
in Hamburg, Germany